SEVEN MINDFUL QUESTIONS

STOP WASTING TIME
REDIRECT YOUR MIND
FOCUS ON WHAT MATTERS

LISA NEZNESKI

Seven Mindful Questions

ISBN-13: 978-1-7347457-4-0

www.529bookdesign.com

SEVEN MINDFUL QUESTIONS

LISA NEZNESKI

HEALTHY MINDFUL SELF

For Edward C. Schatz, V. and George Henry Schatz,
who always ask good questions.
Keep asking questions, sons.

Note to the Reader

In the way that *Grounded in Chaos: Leaning into Adversity, Learning Joy,* gives you hope to survive whatever life throws at you, *Seven Mindful Questions* provides the tools to be more engaged in your everyday life. Asking myself these questions has allowed me to be more effective as a friend, employee, pet parent, teacher, and consultant. (Oh yeah, Mom and Grandmawm, too. Did I just forget my kids?) Whether change is thrust upon you or you choose it, the 7MQ teach you mindfulness on and off the cushion and how to bring your full attention to your interactions with others.

This is your journey.
Nothing is different until you are.
Keep asking questions.

INTRODUCTION

I don't want to miss my life!
(That one time when I almost died.)

I'm in the UPMC Presby Emergency Room.
I'm hooked up to monitors.
I'm there because of horrendous chest pain.
The pain starts between my shoulder blades.
The sensation of a knife blade,
Being knifed in the back,
Pulses and crescendos.
I watch the pulsation and the peaks on the monitor.
As the pain increases,
My heart rate goes from 50 to 40.
I say out loud to no one in particular, "Watch the monitor."
Heads turn to the screen.
Some are watching the EKG, Oxygen Saturation.
It takes them all a second to recognize that.
As the pain gets worse,
My heart rate drops.
I say out loud, "My pulse is dropping."
As the pain worsens, my heart rate continues to drop
From 40 to 38, 36, 32.
Perplexed faces watch
To see if I go pulseless.
I'm awake and watching myself fade
And I say out loud,
"Tell the kids I love them,
This could be it.

I don't want to miss my life."
I am well aware that I really could be dying,
Before anyone else is aware.
And the room fills with medical personnel,
Watching the spectacle of the heart rate dropping below 30.
Around 28, I take a deep breath.
The pain subsides and the heart rate starts to climb.
The rhythm returns to normal,
Cardiac enzymes normal—no heart attack.
No need for the chaos of the medical resuscitation
Known as cardiac arrest.
Pain pendulating.
This cycle of pain leading to a deathly low heart rate
Repeats about four times,
Until they call the Cardiologist.
The on-call Cardiologist is the guy
Who shares the very same birthday as me.
I know him because
I'm on four blood pressure medications,
And my blood pressure remains high.
We are kindred, stressed-out medical professionals.
My medication regimen, four high-power pills,
A very clear indicator that my body has
Way too much stress.
Four blood pressure medications,
And I'm somewhere in my mid-fifties.
Until that day, with chest pain,
When my Cardiologist admits me
For observation,

I swear to him that I did not take the
Blocker known as labetalol,
The one that lowers heart rate.
I swear I hadn't taken it for two weeks.
He says it could be third-spaced,
Meaning it is slowly coming out of my tissues.
—We speak in technical terms
Because we respect each other's knowledge base—
Coming out of my body slowly
And still having an effect,
Which is as plausible an explanation
As anything else at this point,
Because they have no idea
What the fuck is going on.

It came on very, very strangely.
My very first grandchild was born
The night before.
In the summer of 2014,
I left an extremely stressful job
And started working for my present employer
Just two weeks prior.
I had everything to look forward to.
I went out to a special lunch
At the "Ditka's" restaurant
To celebrate the birth.
Ditka's is a $100 lunch,
So, it was a really special occasion.
While sitting there,

Congratulating my new grandmother-hood,
It came on so suddenly—
Knife-like chest pain and severe nausea—
That I went to the ladies' room
To catch my breath.
I inverted myself and
Hung upside down from the waist.
Trying to stretch,
And I began retching.
Really? I never even puked
When I was pregnant.
I am so sick that I didn't even eat.
I asked for my $100 Ditka's lunch to go. Really.
I went to the chiropractor for an adjustment.
I took a muscle-relaxant.
And, at three o'clock in the morning,
I stopped waiting and analyzing
And ended up in the ER.
The rest of the day was a blur.
The only clear thought I had was:
I don't want to miss my life.

Imagine if I had toughed it out,
A well-grooved habit of ignoring my body.
Imagine having your body scream
At you to pay attention
With an extremely dramatic,
Sad, and very slow heart rate.
Me wide awake,

Me reading the monitor,
Me seeing and understanding
What was happening
Before anyone else in the room.
Pain equals rapid decline and very unsafe heart rate.
This was no whisper to pay attention,
This was a
"WAKE THE FUCK UP, LISA" primal scream.
From deep in my soul.

The day I find out that my grandson
Came into this world,
Came into this life,
I'm about to check out. And,
"I don't want to miss my life."
Fucking Augenblick.

Augenblick

Augenblick n.(lit) "in the blink of an eye," a "decisive moment in time" that is fleeting, yet momentarily eventful and incredibly significant.

Have you ever had a moment of Augenblick? Think back to one moment that was pivotal, one moment that changed your life "in the blink of an eye," or that moment that felt significant yet fleeting. What I find so meaningful about Augenblick is that you need to be present—be in the moment to appreciate that incredibly significant moment. That is the essence of mindfulness. Being present in the moment for "what is" happening right then and there. Not all moments in life are of the happy Augenblick kind or like the dramatic-in-the-ER Augenblick kind. Most moments are just mundane, routine, regular, everyday kind of moments. You don't have to experience an "I don't want to miss my life" moment like I did to experience an Augenblick moment. My body brought me to the brink of annihilation (a few times) before I pivoted and made the changes needed to realign my focus and integrate my body, mind, and spirit.

That is one of the main goals of mindfulness. You don't have to get to that point to uncover the secret to mindfulness. My goal here is to show you that if you can be present for making coffee, folding the laundry, sweeping the floor, making your bed, or brushing your teeth, you are primed, ready, and in a state to find your Augenblick moments. Being present and truly being in the moment—that's mindfulness.

In Seven Mindful Questions, we'll explore how to be present in our everyday lives, so when a moment of Augenblick comes along, you are ready to appreciate it and not miss your life. The Seven Mindful Questions is a tool I've created to help you succeed. Studying mindfulness meditation can enhance the application of the Seven Mindful Questions—although you need not have any background in mindfulness or meditation to benefit from the regular use of these questions. In fact, coming to the Seven Mindful Questions with no previous experience in mindfulness may be a wide-open gateway into mindfulness because you have no preconceived notions. However, the Seven Mindful Questions are meant for anyone who wants to not miss their life.

The questions are designed to find you where you are, wake or shake you up a bit, and increase your personal presence. Personal presence is a toe in the water of Augenblick moments. Personal presence is bringing your whole self (body, mind, and spirit) to the task at hand; it's about interacting with others without getting lost in your own thoughts; it's about being aware of your emotions as they arise. People know when you are paying attention to them, just as they know when you are thinking about something other than the conversation, or you're focused on what you're going to say next. Using the Seven Mindful Questions will enhance your ability to stay with whatever is going on—be engaged with people or living beings or the environment in a meaningful way so that you radiate focused attention.

I discovered the word Augenblick in a list of words that do not have a direct translation into English. I used it to describe significant moments where I wrote about the enormous changes in my life in my first book, Grounded in Chaos. Every one of the narrative poems in the Augenblick Section contains a significant moment where I was fully aware, fully present, fully acknowledging the moment as it was happening. The main reason that I have so many moments of Augenblick is that I have been committed to using the Seven Mindful Questions since that day in the ER. That's my hope for you—that you will apply the Seven Mindful Questions in a way that leads you to abounding moments of Augenblick in your life.

SEVEN MINDFUL QUESTIONS

Seven Steps: Three Steps Down, Turn, Three Steps Back

When I was a kid, I lived in a house that had three steps from the kitchen down to the mudroom. Countless times I started down those steps and, by the time I reached the bottom, did a U-turn and went right back up, as if I'd forgotten something. Three steps down, pause, turn, three steps back: Seven steps total.

Even though I no longer lived in that house, I grooved a habit of running those steps in my mind and changing direction when needed. I noticed that it took me three steps before I would wake up, pay attention, and correct my course. Not long after I was in the hospital with the low heart rate, I started to check in with myself regularly so that I wouldn't miss my life. The check-ins evolved into this seven-step process, using the Seven Mindful Questions. I found that my seven-step habit was helping me cope with working full-time, with relationships, health challenges, and the demands of living through these unprecedented times.

This habit, along with a robust daily mindfulness meditation practice, has become my North Star. I can count on this habit to make sense of my life and propel me forward. Using the Seven Mindful Questions as a complement to my meditation practice, has increased my ability to be in the now; meaning, I discovered that being present creates personal presence, which is an unstoppable positive force. Who doesn't want that?

When I began using the Seven Mindful Questions to reclaim my life, I recognized that my mindfulness practice had centered around strategic pauses and continuous negotiations—a back and forth akin to running the steps. So, to gain clarity and direction, when I'd reach that point of feeling on the edge because of too much to do and too little time to do it in, I started running the steps of the Seven Mindful Questions. Each step downward challenges you to look inwardly, pause, and make a decision. When it was hard to quiet my mind, to get clarity, to be in the present moment, I started running the steps.

You will find that as you start to pay attention, lots of things will scream for your attention. Thoughts randomly pop into your head as you practice. But is that thought important enough to be acted on? I began to use the Seven Mindful Questions in conjunction with my mindfulness meditation practice. I had a real heart-to-heart with myself after one particularly "busy mind meditation." I said, "Look, Lisa, you can allow those 'super important thoughts' that pop into your meditation to interrupt the practice or flow into a parking lot. Stop worrying that you'll forget them after meditation is over!

Stop attaching. Stop reacting. If it's really that important, trust yourself. You will think this 'super important thought' again at the right time. It's just a thought, nothing else."

After that realization, I found the fascinating cyclical influence of the Seven Mindful Questions impacting my mindfulness meditation practice, and it got easier. Because I had the Seven Mindful Questions at the ready for getting back into the day, I could focus on calming my mind, body, and spirit during the practice. I'm jumping ahead a bit but using the Seven Mindful Questions was the door to tremendous insight and realization. Combining mindfulness meditation with well-established good questioning techniques opened new doors of possibilities, heightened my body awareness and my desire to heal, and increased my productivity exponentially.

Mindfulness combined with the Seven Mindful Questions will help you in countless ways, too, specifically if you:

- are working from home and managing work, children, a spouse, and general day-to-day life
- are flummoxed by competing priorities
- wonder how you will get everything done personally and professionally
- are an individual contributor and manage your own schedule
- work in teams, where each person has responsibilities for their part of the project

- need more structure
- have trouble developing or keeping a routine
- want to improve your emotional intelligence
- are committed to improving yourself
- want to show up as a better version of yourself every day
- and, most importantly, you want to see what really matters

Can you see yourself in at least one of the above situations? I see myself in all of them. The Seven Mindful Questions was written with you in mind. I take to heart what Richard Bach meant when he said: *"We teach best what we most need to learn."* If you are willing to put in the work, the benefits of using the Seven Mindful Questions can bring personal presence into your life and jumpstart the process of living mindfully—and you will reap all the benefits of intentional living and discover the joy of what really matters.

If you're wondering what mindfulness is and how it can relate to your daily life, this book will attempt to demystify it from a meditative practice to simply living in the present moment with the Seven Mindful Questions. The overarching goal of mindfulness is to return you to "now." Now. With the imperative that now brings. Without procrastination. Or excuses. With a sense of supreme self-compassion. Let's get started. Are you ready to try?

The Seven Mindful Questions:

1. What am I doing right now? (Awareness)
2. Why am I doing this at all? (Because)
3. Why do I care about this? (Care)
4. ★Pause and breathe.★ What else should I be doing? (Pause)
5. Choose: What is essential? (Choose)
6. What can I do better? (Better)
7. What is the best alternative? (Alternative)

Aware, Because, Care, Pause and Breathe, Choose, Better, Alternative (ABC-Pause-CBA)
I'm Aware Because I Care.
★Pause and Breathe.★
I Choose a Better Alternative.

The Seven Mindful Questions, just like the stairs, are three steps down, turn, and go back up in reverse order (ABC-Pause-CBA). Each step of the Seven Mindful Questions takes you deeper into the process until you make a conscious decision to purposefully turn in the right direction without backtracking or repeating yourself. The seven questions build on one another, challenging you to pay attention, gauging your actions against what you value.

Each question has an entire chapter devoted to a deep dive, so let's take an introductory look at the questions. At first, the questions seem simple, and admittedly they are, but they are designed to catch yourself in mindless action so that you can redirect into purposeful mindful behavior. The first three questions are the thump on the noggin to get you to be more present, more aware of your actions and the meaning behind them. Let's focus on those.

Step One, Question One: "What am I doing right now?" This brings your actions into awareness.

"Awareness" is the first step. Noticing and being aware of what you are doing is a doorway to mindfulness.

Step Two, Question Two: "Why am I doing this?" This is the big "Because."

All behavior is purposeful, so it naturally follows that there should be a "Because." The reason behind your action may be conscious or entirely subconscious; however, there is a purpose to what you are doing. We will strive to make the subconscious overt so that you can be consciously aware of this "why."

Step Three, Question Three: "Why do I care about this?" This question challenges you to look at what you value and what you care about. Do you care about "the reason" you are doing the action? Answering this question will help you get a deeper understanding of the emotional need behind your action.

These first three steps form the foundation of the process. Awareness, Because, Care: ABC. Simple, right? Using the mnemonic "I'm Aware Because I Care" focuses your attention on the now. Although easy to remember, mindful awareness requires practice, and eventually, you'll start to recognize that you are spending time on what gives your life meaning.

Let's look at the remaining sequence of questions, which round out the Seven Mindful Questions and bring us "back up the stairs" with a fresh point-of-view. Once you've asked the first three questions or taken the first three steps, Question Four is the turning point where you pause and breathe.

Step Four, Question Four, leads you to think about the other options you have: "What else should I be doing?" At this point, I'm usually thinking of a dozen other things that I could be doing: But which one *should* I be doing? Which task has the highest priority? It is amazing how quickly we can shuffle priorities and recognize the high-value tasks when we're open and honest.

Step Five, Question Five: "Choose: What is essential?" is asking you to take action. As you begin to think strategically about your choices, about what is realistic and manageable, about what you can get done in the time you have, the essential tasks reveal themselves. As what is essential begins to take on new meaning, not just task oriented, you start to think about making time for yourself and time for self-care. As my mindful meditation practice deepened, I found that "choosing what's essential" challenges me to have self-compassion and take better care of myself.

Step Six, Question Six: "What can I do better?" creates a foundational framework based on what you value. If you've made a conscious choice, it's easy to be compassionate with yourself if the day goes sideways or you don't get tasks done.

Step Seven, Question Seven, brings the cycle of self-negotiation to a natural conclusion by asking: "What is the best alternative?" Having an awareness of your priorities refocuses your point of view.

I sometimes rephrase that question to "What is the most important thing for me to be doing right now?" But the essence of examining what matters to you is totally captured with "What is the best alternative?"

What matters to you? The Seven Mindful Questions will help you become more present, focus your time on what's important, decrease wasting time, develop more self-awareness and self-compassion, and point you toward your North Star—meaning your true purpose. If you, like me, don't want to miss your life, the check-ins with the Seven Mindful Questions will bring you right back up the stairs to what the now means to you.

Becoming aware of what you are doing, especially if it's taking away time from what you value, can be mind-blowing and life-changing. Mastering the process of asking yourself the sequential self-examination questions in the *Seven Mindful Questions*, like mindfulness, may take a lifetime. But putting the Seven Mindful Questions into practice is as simple as learning your ABCs. The entire sequence takes just a few seconds.

I'm Aware Because I Care. ★Pause and Breathe.★ I Choose a Better Alternative.

As your guide, I will gently lead you through the process of self-discovery built on the Seven Mindful Questions (7MQ). Although your answers will be different than mine, I'm certain this method will guide you into self-realization, too. With continued use, the 7MQ method will propel you forward, and you will begin to live mindfully, on purpose, and bring your best self to your everyday life.

Let's find your moments of Augenblick and make the most of them.

What Is Mindfulness?

*"The real meditation practice is how we live our lives
from moment to moment to moment."*

—Jon Kabat-Zinn

What if I were to tell you that you could have a much
more meaningful life just by paying attention? There was
a point in my life when all I could "pay" was attention.
When you're lying on that cold, uncomfortable
emergency room gurney, the only thing in the world that
matters is what is happening right then and there. After
the emergency room episode, things went from bad to
worse. I was a broke-ass, rundown, at-my-wits-end, old
lady. So, I reached down into that empty change-purse of
a life and paid what I could. I paid attention.

I've always loved a good challenge. So, in the middle
of a stressful separation from my then-husband, I
committed to a 60-Day Meditation Challenge that
practiced selective attention for about five minutes every
day. Honestly, that's all you need to begin a mindfulness
practice: five minutes. Mindfulness is selectively directing
your attention to the present moment. I still had a

demanding job, and I still had responsibilities. The world wasn't going to stop because I was divorcing. Day by day, a little at a time, I developed a mindfulness habit that began with selectively paying attention for just five minutes a day.

I began to explore mindfulness through selective attention both during meditation and in my daily life. The simplest definition of mindfulness is being fully present in the moment. We really only have what is happening in the present moment. Now. Only now. Not yesterday or tomorrow, but right now.

There was a time that I hopped in my car and, sixty miles later, I pulled into the parking lot of the hospital with absolutely no recollection of the drive. It was like I was teleported. Has this ever happened to you? If you've ever driven to work and all you remember is getting into the car and arriving at work, you've been lost in thought, too. Being lost in thought is the antithesis of mindfulness. There are actions that we all do that don't require supreme concentration or conscious thought: your heart beats, your lungs breathe, your kidneys filter, your body lives without your conscious direction. (That's the way it was designed, and we will come back to that in a bit.) What if, instead of zoning out, you began to pay attention to what you're doing right now? What if, on that drive to work, you noticed the colors of the sky, the trees, the size of the trucks going by, the bits of trash by the side of the road, that pothole near mile marker 25, and countless other details? If you are going through every day without paying attention and being lost in thought, you're missing out on the best parts of being alive.

Mindfulness training allows you to find the meaning in the moment. According to Janice Marturano, founder of the Institute for Mindful Leadership and author of *Finding the Space to Lead*, learning mindfulness techniques can teach you ". . . clarity, focus, creativity, and compassion." I like to say mindfulness fundamentals teach compassion for yourself and others, provide clarity, improve focus, and spark creativity.

Mindfulness takes a step back and looks at the unconscious body mechanisms and asks: How does it feel to breathe? What do you hear right now? What does your body feel like right now? These questions make the unconscious conscious. Those are the three anchors to a mindfulness meditation practice: the breath, listening to your surroundings, and sensations in your body. Paying attention to one of these three aspects as a beginning meditator allows you to train your mind to be in the present moment by making the unconscious conscious.

What does it mean to be in the present moment? For most of my life, I've spent my time in thinking mode. It paid off, and I created a successful career based on my ability to reason and my intellect. But thinking alone does not make a successful life. Being in thinking mode allowed me to tune out all the distractions in a busy nursing home and focus on the patient's medications back when I was a consultant pharmacist. There would be patients calling out, feeding pumps beeping, medication carts rolling around, lunch trays being delivered, and a high level of ambient noise. I would go into my thinking zone and tune all of it out so that I could perform my work. The side-effect of being able to tune out the ambient noise is that you can't turn it back on very easily, which resulted in my sons having to say "Mom, Mom, Mom, Mom, Mom" five times in rapid-fire succession to get my attention. I would wake up by the fourth "Mom," but only hear the last one. Tragic but true. The more stressful my life became, the more I retreated into my head. My body suffered. I wasn't taking good care of my body, mind, or spirit. Four blood pressure medications were just one symptom of an unbalanced, stressed-out life. Something had to change. So, thinking mode is not the present moment. Thinking mode, lost-in-thought mode, is not the present moment. Waking up to what is happening in your body and in your surroundings—and paying attention to it—is the beginning of mindfulness.

Present moment awareness is bringing your full self, your body and your mind, to the same place at the same time. It is the exact opposite of multi-tasking. I used to take pride in my ability to multi-task. And there have been times when I absolutely needed to split my attention. But having your attention split is not sustainable. Eventually, nothing is done very well, and you feel pulled in multiple directions, exponentially increasing your stress level.

Have you ever forgotten about something in the washer to find it days later, stinking, needing to be rewashed? That's just one example of multi-tasking gone bad. And, whether you consciously know it or not, your body begins to store that stress. I stored that stress and didn't deal with it directly until the most neglected thing started screaming for my attention: my whole body. My deathly slow heart rate grabbed my full attention. The pendulum had swung the other way, and I had to stop all the one-sided attention that was on my future and the *what-ifs* and rebalance. Mindfulness was one of the techniques I used to accomplish this. When you give something your full attention, thoughts, feelings, and sensations in your body are all balanced.

This brings me back to the Seven Mindful Questions. Using the questions in the ABC-Pause-CBA sequence is the tool you can use to achieve the balance you're seeking by making the unconscious conscious. Instead of rushing headlong through life, the 7MQ give space to examine thoughts, feel the emotions, and gauge the impact on your body. The 7MQ provide the personal presence to not miss your life while it is happening.

Guided Meditation: Mindfulness of the Breath

You may find it helpful to experience mindfulness with this simple guided meditation. Using the 7MQ can be enhanced with this meditation as an adjunct to your learning. This short meditation is available to download at https://www.lisanezneski.com/seven-mindful-questions-meditations. However, if it's not convenient to download, you may find it helpful to use a voice recorder and record your own voice so that you can follow along with the cues.

• • •

Settle into your chair. For this exercise, it might be easiest to practice sitting with your feet flat on the floor. I invite you to take a few deep breaths. Breathe deeply into your belly. You may want to place a hand on your belly and feel the rise and fall. When it feels right, as you breathe, you may close your eyes or cast your eyes downward to limit visual distraction. Continue to take at least two more deep breaths, fully inflating your lungs, and then begin to breathe naturally.

Take several natural breaths. Now, focus on where the breaths enter your body at the tip of your nostrils. Feel the entire breath cycle as the air enters your nose, fills your lungs, and leaves your body. For the next minute, pay attention to how the breath enters your nose, fills your lungs, and exits.

—Allow yourself a full minute to remain quiet, focusing on the breath—

If your attention wanders away from your breath, acknowledge the wandering, and gently bring your attention back to your breath.

—Allow yourself 30 seconds and remain quiet—

Now, bring your attention to the length of your inhale. Now, try to make the exhale just a little longer than the inhale. For example, inhale for four seconds and exhale for five. By exhaling a bit longer, you activate the body's natural relaxation mechanism, the parasympathetic nervous system. Don't force your breaths, just let the exhale go longer naturally.

—Allow yourself 30 seconds to bring your attention to the exhale, letting it be longer than the inhale—

Slowly bring your attention back to the room, your attention back to your body, wiggle your fingers or your toes, and stretch a bit. When comfortable and ready, you may open your eyes.

Congratulate yourself for taking time for yourself today.

• • •

Sunset

I almost missed it.
The dog, Oshie, wanted to go outside.
It was not quite dusk, but yet it was twilight.
I made small talk with the neighbors,
Walked around the front yard,
And went to pull the trash can to the street.
There I was, task-oriented: walk the dog, take out the trash.
As I turned, trash can handle in hand,
I looked up and stopped dead in my tracks.
There, above me
The most beautiful colors of the sunset
Took my breath away.
I stopped in my tracks,
Handle in hand.
I almost missed it.
Looking up to appreciate, I saw
The clouds were a blue-gray.
The sky was streaked with pink bands between the clouds.
A bright streak of yellow sat near the horizon,
And the blue sky between the clouds
Was the blue of the fake sky in the Las Vegas Venetian.
So that's where they got the color.
That color of blue is real,
It's not "fake blues,"
And I'm seeing it.
Totally out of my task-oriented routine,
I began to walk Oshie around the neighborhood.

Mostly so I could appreciate the last moments of light,

The colors changed and morphed so rapidly.

I turned around toward the east and looked back at night.

I looked off toward the west and, again,

Watched the pink streaks change,

Dropping lower and lower,

Until the pink touched the yellow at the horizon.

For five simple minutes,

I took a pause to breathe

And appreciate the beauty of nature around me.

Red sky at night.

Tomorrow's going to be a good day.

And I was there to appreciate it.

QUESTION ONE:
AWARE

The Seven Mindful Questions:

1. **What am I doing right now? (Awareness)**
2. Why am I doing this? (Because)
3. Why do I care about this? (Care)
4. ⋆Pause and Breathe.⋆ What else should I be doing? (Pause)
5. Choose: What is essential? (Choose)
6. What can I do better? (Better)
7. What is the best alternative? (Alternative)

I'm Aware Because I Care.
⋆Pause and Breathe.⋆
Choose the Better Alternative.

Awareness

"If you don't ask the right questions, you don't get the right answers. A question asked in the right way often points to its own answer. Asking questions is the ABC of diagnosis. Only the inquiring mind solves problems."

—Edward Hodnett
The Art of Problem Solving:
How to Improve Your Methods

Question One: What am I doing right now?
Entirely by accident, I discovered that I think in questions. I was peeling carrots when a voice inside my head asked: *"How are you?"* You know when you're in the middle of something and you have to stop doing it to answer someone—usually in the other room—and it's irritating? That was my initial reaction. This happened when my life was sliding downward, when I was flat broke and could only afford to "pay attention." But I must have been in a receptive state brought on by the repetitive action of peeling because, when I heard the question, I had to stop peeling carrots and put the knife down. A little irritated, I set my hands on the counter and responded: *"How the hell do you think I'm doing?"*

Little did I realize, this was a pivotal moment that launched me into carefully watching, observing, and examining how I thought and how I felt from that day on. This first check-in would go on to inspire the Seven Mindful Questions.

As I began to pay attention to my inner thoughts, I discovered some startling insights. Kids ask a lot of questions. Adults don't. When did I stop asking questions out loud? At some point during adulthood, my internal dialogue turned into a string of questions. When did that happen? I think in questions. How long have I been doing this? All behavior serves some purpose, and, as I realized the art of question-craft came with tremendous benefits, I started using it to figure out how I got so far off track.

Here is what I realized: We are all natural-born questioners. Our inquisitive mind helps us learn about the world around us. Children ask some of the most provocative questions. They haven't learned to filter themselves yet. My kids grew up in the pre-Google era (if you can even imagine such a time).

One bright afternoon around 1993, I was playing in the backyard with my son, George, who was about three or four years old at the time. He asked me four questions in rapid fire: "Why is the sky blue? What is steel made of? What makes wood strong? Why don't clouds fall down?" He asked them so fast I couldn't think. I was in "parent trouble." You know that feeling when your kids are deeper thinkers than you are, and you have no idea how to answer with half the clarity with which they inquired? Children are naturally in the present moment. Adults, over time, lose that sense of wonderment about bright blue skies and clouds that appear to defy gravity. I have a clear memory of that day and my amazement at how fast his mind worked. It is only in retrospect that I can see how present my son was in his everyday life at four years old. By watching and really seeing the world around him, he had an insatiable sense of wonder and awareness. His observations led naturally to inquiry. Observation is awareness. Awareness cracks open the door to mindfulness.

I found the following quote by Peter Matthiessen on my Zen daily calendar. I think it sums up what I'm trying to convey here. *"Soon the child's clear eye is clouded over by ideas and opinions, preconceptions, and abstractions. Simple free being becomes encrusted with the burdensome armor of the ego. Not until years later does an instinct come that a vital sense of mystery has been withdrawn. The sun glints through the pines and the heart is pierced in a moment of beauty and strange pain, like a memory of paradise. After that day, we become seekers."*

Let's become seekers. What's second nature to me may feel awkward to you, so we're going to take this in baby steps. I want to give you the opportunity to warm up to all seven questions individually. This is not a Boston freeway, where you have to enter traffic at sixty miles an hour just to keep up. This is where I meet you where you are, and you walk with me through the basic techniques that get you into the practice of asking the Seven Mindful Questions.

In social interactions, it's much safer to stick to questions that elicit factual answers. When small talk is required, we naturally ask close-ended questions that lead to limited information based on everyone's comfort level. The classic Pittsburgh question (bad grammar and all) is: "Where are you from?" This is Pittsburghese for safe small talk.

An open-ended question is designed to elicit a longer response than a single word or phrase. These are the types of questions used in the Seven Mindful Questions. They require more creativity and a higher level of thinking to respond. Open-ended questions are inherently evocative. Open-ended questions are a metacognitive skill and can be learned, honed, and practiced. The term "metacognitive" is the higher-order skill of thinking about thinking. In our case, we'll call it questioning that leads to deeper questions. A rightly timed open-ended question can bring us into the present and crack open the door to feeling in the now.

In the quote at the beginning of this chapter, I'm fairly certain that Edward Hodnett did not plan on his "ABC" being an acronym. I think he meant questions are the fundamental method of deeper inquiry. His ABC works—"*. . . Asking questions of yourself is the ABC—I'm Aware Because I Care—of diagnosis. Only the inquiring mind solves its own problems.*" It does seem to fit, doesn't it?

Question One: "What am I doing right now?" is meant to stop you in your tracks and observe.

Let's jump into the exercises on awareness.

Exercises #1, #2, and #3 Awareness

Each of the exercises in this book are composed of three sections: The Instructions, the Exercise, and Reflections. The intentional repetition is there to make sure the Instructions are clear for successful completion. The Reflections are meant to be a point of discovery; reflect on what you are to learn from the exercise and what you learned about yourself in the process.

Awareness of Your Personal Core Foundation

I want you to get comfortable with asking yourself open-ended questions. It is less risky to ask these of yourself. Your internal interrogative dialogue is yours alone. I want you to become better at asking the questions that lead to deep awareness and tough answers. Mostly, I want you to get comfortable with asking questions that evoke feelings. Lean into them and breathe. Feel the emotions that a hard question brings up. Learning everyday mindfulness with the Seven Mindful Questions is a journey into asking better questions to understand your emotions—so you can live a more fulfilled life.

I find it helpful to think of the Seven Mindful Questions as a self-negotiation process that deepens self-awareness. Question One introduced Awareness. However, to properly set the stage for using the Seven Mindful Questions, it's important to understand what you value to begin appreciating the "now." This will help you discover your Personal Core Foundation.

What do you want out of life?

Why do you want it?

Your vision must be crystal-clear. This exercise is designed to help you know yourself at a deeper level than you thought possible. Knowing your thoughts, dreams, and passions, and acknowledging your subconscious desires that drive your conscious actions, is the level of mindful awareness we are striving to achieve. Awareness of your "drivers" can steer you to the most rewarding journey of your life while being kind to yourself for past mistakes.

Instructions for Exercise #1: Getting Comfortable with "The Questions"

Let's get warmed up. Here's a preliminary exercise to get your juices flowing. The purpose of this exercise is to ask some basic questions to begin the process of thinking about your life. These are your "How are you?" Exercises

#1, #2, and #3. (These are best done altogether, so block out about twenty minutes.)

Get out a blank piece of paper and get ready to answer the question in Exercise #1. You have ten minutes. Set a timer and go. If you need more time, write until your mind is empty. If you don't have paper handy, use your electronic device or spend ten minutes thinking about this question. I prefer going old school and believe there is something magic about committing your answers to paper but do whatever feels right for you.

Exercise #1: Getting Comfortable with "The Questions"

Set a timer for ten minutes and use the prompts to answer this question:

What would my fulfilled life look like?

Visualize everything in a world where your dreams are all fulfilled and describe it in as much detail as possible.

Here are a few prompts to get you thinking:

- Where are you living?
- What line of work are you in?
- What are your hobbies?
- Who is sharing your life with you?
- What does an average day look like?
- How are you spending your time?

Keep in mind that your first thoughts may be top-of-mind obligations. Dare to dream of a life of joy. We are meant to live a life of joy.

Exercise #2: Getting Comfortable with "The Answers"

The purpose of this exercise is to get comfortable with the feelings brought on by the answers to those questions. Imagine yourself living that fulfilled life.

How would you feel living every aspect of your fulfilled life?

Now, take out another piece of blank paper and lay it next to your answers from Exercise #1.

Close your eyes, breathe into it, and visualize how the answer to each question feels. See yourself actually living it. Visualize yourself living a life focused on what matters to you. If the word *joy* comes to mind, spend a couple of minutes feeling it in your heart and visualizing it. Get creative. You may want to draw an image or paint a representative color or journal about the emotions in the vision. Then, document the feeling next to each answer from Exercise #1.

Close your eyes and breathe. Then, write the first feeling that comes to mind without editing next to each answer. Write, draw, paint, or journal about how you feel. Take as long as you need for each response to feel complete.

Exercise #3: Your Personal Core Foundation

Let's clarify and define your Personal Core Foundation. Continue using your answers from Exercise #1 and #2 to take a deeper look at six important areas. Spend time reflecting on what matters to you in the following areas:

- Relationships – All the people in your life
- Homelife – Where and how you are living
- Work Life – All the aspects of your work life that are fulfilling
- Financial Obligations – How you are able to meet your responsibilities
- Spiritual Life – How you connect with your Higher Power
- Health – Your ability to maintain good health

Close your eyes, breathe into it, and visualize how it feels to be living your fulfilled life in each of these areas. These are my six pillars of my Personal Core Foundation. Feel free to add or modify to fit your priorities. Spend a few minutes feeling the emotion and then journal, draw, paint, or whatever comes to mind.

Reflections on Exercises #1, #2, and #3

How successful were you in imagining your life and experiencing the feelings that go with it? You might want to do these exercises every day for a week to see how your vision evolves. Rather than trying to force an answer in ten minutes, let your subconscious work it out. A vision accompanied by a compelling emotion is a powerful and motivating force.

Your circumstances may change, people may come and go, jobs evolve, but the pillars of your Personal Core Foundation in each area of your life will remain constant. My six pillars are relationships, homelife, work life, financial obligations, spiritual development, and good health. Each of the 7MQ will be bounced up against your Personal Core Foundation. By keeping your focus on what matters, you won't miss your life.

I can tell you from experience, the vision of my fulfilled life becomes clearer each time I do these exercises. Most of the time, I go past the time allotted. Sometimes, I get stuck. There are times when I find a bit of resistance to appreciating a certain item on the list. I know to explore the "item of resistance" in prayer or meditation.

When you *link the vision to a positive emotion* and see yourself living that fulfilled life in your mind's eye, things begin to line up and, without much effort, doors begin to open. With regular use of the 7MQ, you will need less effort to live in alignment with your Personal Core Foundation. These three exercises are good for you, like sauerkraut for breakfast. (Weird Al's mother fed him sauerkraut for breakfast and said, "It's good for you.")

In addition to bringing up positive emotions, these exercises may also bring up self-critical, negative emotions. No judgment here. Trust me, and mindfulness will help you develop self-compassion, which we will discuss with Question Four: Pause and Breathe. This book is not meant to be a substitute for professional help. If you are feeling strong negative emotions or extreme negative feelings that may be unhealthy, contact a doctor, therapist, or counselor trained to help you. I encourage you to get the professional help you need.

Your Personal Core Foundation

Your Personal Core Foundation is what matters most to you. These exercises dipped your toe into the thought-provoking waters by examining what matters and how you feel about it.

My faith in God is the rock for my Personal Core Foundation, and my Personal Core Foundation is my purpose in life—the place I return to when all routine and normality have been blown away. When it gets down to it, living your life around what matters is mindfulness in action. With 7MQ as your guide, you'll "question" your way into a mindful life, and there will be a natural falling away of the unimportant.

As you gain proficiency through practice, you'll start to feel comfortable using these questions daily. At first it will be consciously, and then gradually it will become automatic like a reflex, asking questions as the process becomes second nature. Properly framed questions will allow you to get to the bottom of what you really want to do with your life.

When Question One, "What am I doing right now?" is asked in relation to what your fulfilled life might look like, it aligns what you're doing with what you value. This question is meant to stop you in your tracks mid-task. It starts the process of redirecting your actions to things you value, things that matter.

I think the repetitive action of peeling carrots put me in a receptive state that is like the state of mindful awareness in meditation. When I listened to the question and stopped peeling those carrots, I realized my life was completely off track and I was nowhere near my core foundation. The ups, downs, out-of-control gut-wrenching inevitable change was long overdue. I wasn't even near the nadir of my life at that point—in fact, I was at the top of the roller coaster where you hit the peak of that slow ascent and can look down at what is coming. On that carrot peeling day, I was looking down at the ride of my life, complete with inversions and turns taken at 60 miles per hour.

I recently stood underneath the Hulk Rollercoaster at Islands of Adventure in Orlando. I watched the coaster do flips, turns, and inversions. The entire ride was less than a minute, but I remember thinking, *No fucking way*. I've lived that in technicolor real life. I realized this on the carrot-peeling day, and it changed my life.

Guided Meditation: A Deeper Look Your Personal Core Foundation

This guided meditation focuses on your Personal Core Foundation, answering the question: "What would my fulfilled life look like?" You may want to look back at your answers to the exercises to refresh your memory and set the tone for the meditation. You may find it easier to record the meditation in your own voice and play it back. This meditation is not strictly mindfulness but helps crystallize your Personal Core Foundation.

This short meditation is available for download at: https://www.lisanezneski.com/seven-mindful-questions-meditations.

• • •

Settle into your chair. Sit comfortably with your feet on the floor and your back up against the chair. I invite you to take a few deep breaths. Breathe deeply into your belly. And when the time seems right, I invite you to take a deep breath and, if it's comfortable, on the exhalation, close your eyes or cast your eyes downward to limit visual distraction. In this short meditation, we will visualize everything in a world where your dreams are all fulfilled and describe it in as much detail as possible.

Start by visualizing where you are living. Breathe. Imagine that you see your living space in your mind's eye.

See the outside of your living space. Feel your feet on the ground as you enter your living space. Imagine you are standing to look around and feel the emotion brought on by living in your ideal space. Take several breaths and note where the emotion is felt in your body. Is it your belly or your heart space or somewhere else in your body? Feel the space in your body where the emotion brought on by your ideal living space resides. Sit with this feeling until it feels complete. Breathe.

Next, let's imagine the people in your life. Who are you sharing your life with? Take time to bring to mind your significant others, spouse, children, grandchildren, and friends. Breathe and bring the image of the people you love into your mind's eye. At first, it may be easiest to focus on one beloved person. See yourself enjoying their company. You may be visualizing a holiday, a special occasion, or family gathering. Take as long as you need to visualize yourself interacting with them.

Now take several breaths and note the emotions you feel interacting with people you love. Now feel into the emotions. Take several breaths and note where the emotion is felt in your body. Feel the space in your body where the emotion lives that is brought on by living with and loving significant people in your life. Sit with this feeling until it feels complete. Breathe.

Now imagine your best job ever, whether it's your current employment, a past job, or one that is yet to come. Even if you are not employed, imagine yourself doing work or something that you love. Breathe and bring that image into your mind's eye. Imagine yourself doing the tasks, meeting with colleagues, sharing responsibilities, having productive projects, having meaningful customer or client interactions, or whatever type of work is appropriate to your best job. Or imagine yourself doing something where you bring your best effort. Imagine yourself succeeding in ways that are wildly effective and you are rewarded and compensated well for your efforts.

Spend a few minutes visualizing your ideal job. Take several breaths and note where the sensations and emotions are felt in your body. Feel the space in your body where the emotion brought on by your best job resides. Sit with this feeling until it feels complete. Breathe.

Next, imagine yourself living a fulfilled average day. Imagine yourself waking up and feeling grateful for the day even before your feet hit the floor. Take your time and imagine what an ordinary extraordinary day is like. Add detail to your day, imagining what you are doing and who you are interacting with from the moment of wakefulness to the last moment before you close your eyes for bed. As you imagine each detail, feel the emotion at each point. Feel the emotion of a good nourishing and healthy breakfast. Feel the emotion that accompanies walking the dog or other routine activity. Imagine each ordinary daily activity with new eyes and see the extraordinary in it. Breathe. Imagine a life where your financial responsibilities are easily met. Breathe. Imagine how it feels to have a healthy body. Take a breath between each action and let your day play out like a movie in your mind. Feel the spaces in your body where the emotion brought on by noting the extraordinary in the ordinary resides. Sit with this feeling until it feels complete. Breathe.

Allow yourself several minutes of quiet reflection, gratitude, and connection with your higher power. Allow your mind to rest in open awareness.

Now as we bring this meditation to a close, feel all the wonderful, positive feelings of your Personal Core Foundation. Take several breaths feeling into your whole body and where all the emotions of your Personal Core Foundation live. Feel into your reasons for living and feel the power of a fulfilled life. Sit with this whole-body emotion for a minute.

And gradually, when you are ready, take one more breath, slowly wiggling your fingers and toes. Come back to the room and, when you are ready, you may open your eyes.

• • •

QUESTION TWO:
BECAUSE

The Seven Mindful Questions:

1. What am I doing right now? (Awareness)
2. **Why am I doing this? (Because)**
3. Why do I care about this? (Care)
4. ★Pause and Breathe.★ What else should I be doing? (Pause)
5. Choose: What is essential? (Choose)
6. What can I do better? (Better)
7. What is the best alternative? (Alternative)

I'm Aware Because I Care.
★Pause and Breathe.★
Choose the Better Alternative.

Because

Question Two: "Why am I doing this?"

"Because I said so," says every mom everywhere. That answer might be deflective in dealing with kids, but not really insightful. Question Two rapidly follows Question One: "What am I doing, and why am I even doing this?" The curiosity with which you ask Question Two is meant to be neutral, not accusatory or self-critical. If you ask the question with an accusatory tone, you can't help but feel bad, and that's not the purpose of Question Two. A properly used "why" question can be powerful when used to uncover your current motivation—the Because. As in: "Why am I even doing this in the first place?"

It's worth repeating that all behavior is purposeful. The natural response is "Because" in answering Question Two. As you answer this "why" question, "Because" can give insight into whether you are being purposeful with your action or are purposefully filling your time with meaningless activity.

Sometimes you catch yourself doing something for no good reason. This is one of those blink-blink, "I have no idea why I'm doing this" moments. It is also okay if you blink twice, think about it, and have no "Because." If you have no "Because," see if you are avoiding something. Answering "I don't know" to "Why am I doing this?" may reveal that avoidance. Are you doing something subconsciously to deflect yourself from what may be too difficult to think about and act on? Examining your behavior with this question will reveal your hidden motives because all behavior is purposeful. Whether you have a "Because" or not to this question, you have just taken one step deeper into "Awareness" which is the point.

As you direct "Why am I doing this?" internally, gently, without self-criticism, you can begin to see where your current actions are aligned with your overarching principles, your Personal Core Foundation. This question is meant to take you one step further into awareness. Revealing the motivation behind the current action can lead to a profound reprioritization that is more in line with what you value. At first, my "why" was pretty harsh, as I clearly could see how I contributed to all the problems I was dealing with. Ouch. It's taken quite a while for me to not be so hard on myself. My inner dialogue went from being hypercritical to compassionate, and in doing so, it has opened the door to possibilities I never imagined.

When you get stuck in the self-imprisonment of always doing something in a certain way or always needing to be right, you miss out on better options. Asking a neutrally toned "why" question can reveal your motivations in a dispassionate and accepting way. In essence, the way you approach the Seven Mindful Questions, particularly the "why" questions can be healing and affirming. When you have the present moment awareness of what you are doing and why, the insight this creates is a form of mindfulness—self-discipline and self-modulation. Practicing mindfulness through the 7MQ, encourages you to be there for your life.

Let's jump into the next exercise.

Exercise #4: "Aware" and "Because"
Instructions

Let's see if we can uncover some hidden motivations. To give you some practice in asking the first two questions of the Seven Mindful Questions, it is recommended that you do this exercise while going about your day. You are going to be making a list of what you are doing, with the reason why. Think through: "What was I doing?" and "Why was I doing it?"

Exercise #4 – Getting Comfortable with "Aware" and "Because"

Make a list of seven to ten things that you did with the reason in the format below.

Set a timer for ten minutes. Write your answers out longhand in the following format:

I am (doing "x") because (why are you doing it?).

Reflections on Exercise #4– Getting Comfortable with "Aware" and "Because"

Here are my answers to this exercise:

1. I'm getting the car fixed because the air conditioning is not working and I'm uncomfortable
2. I'm applying lotion because I like the way my skin feels afterward
3. I'm meditating because I need peace and clarity
4. I'm walking Oshie because she needs to pee and I'm responsible for her well-being
5. I'm making coffee because *I like the taste of coffee in the morning*
6. I'm checking work email because I need to stay in touch to perform my job according to my own expectations
7. I'm brushing my teeth because I like how my mouth feels and I want good oral health
8. I'm applying sunscreen because I don't want skin cancer (again)
9. I'm preparing for a meeting tomorrow because I want it to go smoothly, and I want to increase my sales while meeting customer expectations
10. I'm showering because I like to feel clean and refreshed

There is a feeling tone that accompanies each answer that I can relate back to my Personal Core Foundation.

Good health, able to earn a good living, managing responsibilities, and personal enjoyment are all part of my Personal Core Foundation and my fulfilled life.

See if you can sense any feeling tones in your answers and if they relate to your Personal Core Foundation. We will explore this feeling tone in the next chapter, "Care." All behavior is purposeful. And, although I don't show any avoidance in my list, negative motivation, such as not getting skin cancer, can be just as energizing as a positive motivation, such as enjoying a good cup of coffee.

Mindful Spilled Coffee

With an unsteady hand,
I spill my coffee
Every morning.

Is it inattention?
Do I overfill the cup
From inattention?

Or perhaps
It is purposeful overfilling,
So that I
Spill my coffee
Every morning.

Taken from *Grounded in Chaos*, originally published May 2020.

QUESTION THREE:
CARE

The Seven Mindful Questions:

1. What am I doing right now? (Awareness)
2. Why am I doing this? (Because)
3. **Why do I care about this? (Care)**
4. ★Pause and Breathe.★ What else should I be doing? (Pause)
5. Choose: What is essential? (Choose)
6. What can I do better? (Better)
7. What is the best alternative? (Alternative)

I'm Aware Because I Care.
★Pause and Breathe.★
Choose the Better Alternative.

Care

Question Three: "Why do I care about this?"
With this third question, we are going down one more step. After we are aware of what is happening and are attempting to find a reason for doing it, we are consciously evaluating whether this event, task, whatever it is we are doing is worth our time, money, or effort. More importantly, is this action in alignment with our foundation. Can you attach value to the "Aware" and "Because"?

Here are some ways to think about caring. If an action is vital, it is necessary for human life, such as eating and sleeping. These are the involuntary biological imperatives. Essential actions are voluntary and also necessary. Paying the bills and doing the laundry are examples of essential actions that you may need to be scheduled into your day. These are the types of activities where caring is implicit. But vital and essential actions are not the focus of the third question.

"Why do I care about this?" is aimed at those times when you catch yourself doing something that may not have value or be the best use of your time. This is where you determine if the "Because" has meaning or is compelling. Is the reason important enough to continue doing the action?

Caring implies an emotional charge, positive or negative. When you ask, "Why do I care about this?", you are meant to feel the "Because." If you are deriving tremendous joy from an action, or if an action is unpleasant but essential, most likely, you will continue both of these actions. The unpleasant and nonessential actions are those that you will, hopefully, stop doing immediately. There is a tremendous range from unpleasant to pleasant, from nonessential to essential, which makes it difficult to categorically align "caring" to a particular action. This stuff's not black and white; it lands in that middle ground. But it's interesting to note the items you really care about. It's also interesting to note the items you don't care about at all, and how much time they are taking up in your life. Those are the easiest to let go. Become aware of how you feel about the specific things that are taking up your time. Out of the subconscious and into the conscious brings insight. "Awareness" with the reason ("Because") behind it and the extent of "Caring" is that thump on the noggin telling you to make a course correction. I'm Aware Because I Care.

Exercise #5—Aware, Because, Care
Instructions
For the next day, at five different times, stop and ask yourself the first three 7MQ and write out your answers. I

like writing longhand because it engages different parts of your brain. Choose a method (longhand vs. electronic) that is most natural for you. The purpose of this exercise is to practice using the questions at various times throughout the day and thinking through what your actions mean in comparison to your Personal Core Foundation.

Exercise #5—Aware, Because, Care

Ask:

1. What am I doing right now? (Awareness)
2. Why am I doing this at all? (Because)
3. Why do I care about this? (Care)

Write out:

I am (describe the action) because (the reason). I care about (this action) as it is (describe the feeling, or what need it is filling).

Write out this statement at least five times as you catch yourself doing various and random things.

Reflections on Exercise #5 – Aware, Because, Care

Here is a sample of my answers:

1. I am walking Oshie because it's morning and she needs her daily constitutional. I care about walking Oshie because she is my responsibility, and she has been with me through thick and thin. She is my best friend. In reading this, I feel tremendous love and care for her.

2. I am paying credit card bills because I want to keep my balances at zero. I care about this because I am finally getting to the point where my debt is not increasing, and I am tackling all the historical debt I took on in the divorce. In reading this, I am proud of myself for sticking to a major goal of getting out of debt. 2021 is that year.

3. I am writing because I enjoy it and I am passionate about writing. I care about this because I know that when I write every day, my writing is better, and I am gaining proficiency in getting my message out. As Jonathan Milligan says: "Your message matters." In reading this, I get the hit of positive energy in my gut when I'm writing and, after all the gut trauma, it's good to do something that feels good.

4. I am working out because I want to stay in shape. I care about this because I want to be the healthiest I can possibly be, and working out, sweating "putty balls," feels great. I feel sore yet proud of myself for taking care of my body, acknowledging that I live in my head too much. In reading this, I am really sore, but I know it's a good sore. I get excited when my heart rate increases, that my heart is healthy, and my muscles are getting stronger. There is no time like now to be healthy.

5. I am making breakfast because I am hungry. I care about this because I don't get enough protein and scrambled tofu is a great source of protein. I care about this because taking the effort to make a good food choice and prepare and cook it nourishes my body and keeps me healthy. In reading this, I recognize how important feeding my body nourishing food is. Yes, I do scramble tofu. Eating right and at the right time is as important as working out.

Insight on Aware, Because, Care

I think you get the idea that the "Awareness" and the "Because" are the fundamental steps into getting you to pay attention to your actions, your motivation, and why it is important to you. When answering why you care about it, you may find that there is a superficial Care, and a deeper Care—like I don't take the time to meal prep or make good food choices and I live in my head too much. On reflection, I looked at how each answer in Exercise #5 reflected my emotional weather. Reflecting on the "Cares" pulls me back into reflecting on my Personal Core Foundation. You will know when you are in alignment as, like I did, you get that hit of positive emotion. The little "yes" in your body that says, *You, my dear, are doing a good job, and I'm proud of you.* Practice saying that to yourself. "You did a good job, and I'm proud of you."

You may discover that you are filling an emotional need with an action when you answer the "Because." When I'm stressed, I crave salty, crunchy things. The emotional stress-eating of something crunchy is one example of me unconsciously eating. (No judgment here—this is one of my issues.) Is eating the best way to handle stress? I am using food to comfort myself. Whoa, major insight here. This is where kindness kicks in.

The Seven Mindful Questions and this question "Why do I care about this?" particularly is aimed at developing a sensitivity to your emotional weather. This process is designed to hone the skill of evaluating your emotional needs from the perspective of your actions. Since all behavior is purposeful, there may be some subconscious need that you are not addressing or not addressing very well. I'm going to let that sink in. You may be doing something that doesn't address a need, but you are doing it to avoid addressing a need. Double whoa. I spent quite a lot of time ruminating on that.

The question "Why do I care about this?" may highlight an unaddressed emotional need that you bring into conscious awareness. The best way to approach that unaddressed need is with the same gentle kindness and concern that you would give to a beloved person or pet. I've done a lot of work on myself from that day when I vowed, "I don't want to miss my life." I am paying much closer attention to my emotional weather and choosing to directly ask my heart whether it Cares. This has been a fascinating reprioritization of my daily schedule during the pandemic and post-election turmoil.

For that person that needs to hear it: Stop being so hard on yourself! Let that nonsense go.

Beating yourself up over not meeting your own needs is just wasting good energy. A simple "I see this need" is enough. Embrace the awareness of your need and I promise, in using the Seven Mindful Questions, we will figure out the best way to have that need met with kindness and concern.

Practice forgiving yourself.

I highly recommend using the Hawaiian technique of forgiveness, Ho'oponopono, aimed at yourself. This technique is useful for big and small hurts, and especially for big and small trespasses against us. Ho'oponopono repeats the following four phrases until you feel better. "I'm sorry. Please forgive me. Thank you. I love you."

Awareness and acknowledgment of an unfulfilled need is often enough to soften the edges. The clarity you derive from the Because rings true like a clear bell. It's heard with such clarity that there is no other conclusion as to how important it is to you. The Because is obvious. Caring about what you are doing will transition into caring for yourself and others.

From the Healthline blog on emotional needs, "The most common emotional needs include affection, acceptance, validation, autonomy, security, trust, empathy, prioritization, connection, and space."

Emotional needs change over time, shifting priority and focus. With repeated use of "Why do I care about this?" you might find that the original emotional need *has* changed or isn't even there anymore, but yet you are doing something "as if" the original reason still existed.

One of my biggest challenges now is menu planning. There are certain things that I make "as if" I were feeding two growing teenage boys. Those boys are men and have been for a while, and I live thousands of miles from each. But I have yet to make the adjustment to feeding one person in single portions with maybe leftovers for another day—not three quarts of chili that lasts over six months in the freezer. *No bueno.* Of course, I care to eat well, and the motivation to feed myself versus making for others has changed, so the prioritization of "me" has shifted with this change.

The amount of change that is layered on our baseline responsibilities due to the pandemic is overwhelming. I've reprioritized my life goals to focus on the very basics— eating, sleeping, shelter, choosing nourishing food, good water—the very bottom of Maslow's hierarchy of needs pyramid. You may note that these are what I called earlier the vital involuntary biologic imperatives. That's about all I can do in a state of overwhelm. Let yourself off the hook, too. If all you can do is focus on the vital biologic imperatives, well done. Using the Seven Mindful Questions allows me to comfortably choose what is right for me in the moment without being excessively hard on myself. Focusing on how I eat is one of my top five needs, and now that I'm Aware Because I Care about the meal planning, I'm going to work through the Pause and Choose a Better Alternative. I'm turning around and starting to come back up the stairs.

Guided Meditation: Quieting Your Mind

Follow these directions for a guided meditation that begins by focusing on your breath. Breath is one type of anchor to return your attention. Some may find it difficult to pay attention to the breath if there are underlying health concerns with breathing. A second type of anchor may be bodily sensations. You may want to feel the sensation of your body in your chair. Again, some may find it difficult to pay attention to the bodily sensations if pain or other discomfort is an issue. The third type of anchor is paying attention to ambient sounds. You may find this anchor helpful if you are in nature or in a place that has a lot of ambient noise, or if the other anchors become uncomfortable. The choice is yours. Each time where I mention "breath" below, you may substitute the anchor that feels best to you. As thoughts pop into your head, allow them to fade away. If the thought is really important, you will think of it again, I promise you. Let thoughts arise and fall away.

This short meditation is available for download at: https://www.lisanezneski.com/seven-mindful-questions-meditations. An alternative to downloading this meditation is you can record your own voice reading the meditation. That way, you can follow along with the recorded cues, in your own voice. Now let's get ready to meditate.

• • •

Settle into your chair. As you feel your feet on the floor or your bottom in the chair, your back against the chair, I invite you to take a few deep breaths. Breathe deeply into your belly. You may want to place a hand on your belly and feel the rise and fall. When it feels right, as you breathe, you may close your eyes or cast your eyes gently downward to limit visual distractions. Continue to take at least two more deep breaths, and then begin to breathe naturally.

Take several natural breaths. Now focus on where the breaths enter your body, at the tip of your nostrils. Feel the air enter your nose. Feel the air as it fills your lungs and exits your body as you breathe out. For the next minute, breathing naturally, pay attention to how the breath enters your nose, fills your lungs, and exits.

Allow yourself a full minute to remain quiet, focusing on the breath.

For the next several minutes, allow yourself to relax into the rhythm of your body. Thoughts will enter your mind. Allow the thought to rise and fall without attaching to it. If you think of thoughts as a train going by, watch the train go by without getting on the train. If you catch yourself on the train, simply get off.

Allow yourself a full minute to remain quiet, focusing on the breath.

It may be helpful to trace the number 8 in your mind with your breath. Ascending to the top of the 8 on the inhale, turning and descending downward to the bottom of the 8 on the exhale. Feel the slight pause at the end of the inhale and the pause at the end of the exhale.

Allow yourself 30 seconds to focus on the number 8 as you breathe.

Release your attention from the breath and silently note what pops into your awareness. Open your attention to anything in your body or your environment.

Notice any sounds, smells, sensations, or mental imagery as you sit quietly.

Allow yourself 30 seconds as you notice what comes into your open awareness.

As thoughts enter your mind, you may find it helpful to say "thinking, thinking, thinking" to take the focus off the thought and return back to the meditation. Allow the thought to rise and fall away. It is very natural for the mind to think. Don't push the thought away. Gently bring your attention back to your anchor.

Spend several minutes allowing sensations, sounds, or smells to arise, silently noting what arises.

Allow yourself 2 minutes of quiet appreciation of what arises.

Let's bring this meditation to a close with a quote from Sri Nisargadatta Maharaj: "A quiet mind is all you need. All else will happen rightly, once your mind is quiet. As the sun on rising makes the world active, so *does self-awareness affect changes in the mind. In the light of calm and steady self-awareness, inner energies wake up and work miracles without effort on your part."* Now, slowly bring your attention back to the room, your attention back to your body, wiggle your fingers and your toes, stretch a bit and, when comfortable, you may open your eyes. Well done. Thank yourself for and taking time to explore your inner weather today.

• • •

An acknowledgment to Liam McClintock and the Fit Mind Training system for some of the meditation verbiage and phraseology used in this meditation.

LOOKING IN THE MIRROR

A Moment of Self-Reflection: Acknowledge How Far You've Come Before Moving On with the 7MQ

Finding Time for Lisa

How?
How in the world did things get so bad?
How in the world did I get so sick?
Why did I ignore myself?
Did I prioritize everyone else's needs before mine?
How did I let my inattention to my body
Get so far out of whack?
You don't get participation points
For chest pain
When you are lying on the gurney.

I knew deep in my body
That I was in big trouble.
I was ignoring how I was feeling.
My body was screaming for
Attention and
I had to stop ignoring
How I felt.
My Personal Core Foundation
Wasn't working.
I was pushing too hard
In a direction that only I wanted to go.
I had assumed that my health and relationship
Pillars were solid.
They weren't.

Finally, when I realize that living on 10 acres
In the woods, with no neighbors,

Isolated,
Is not healthy.
I make some drastic changes.

With the clarity of sudden awareness,
I know that the relationship pillar had crumbled to dust.
It was as if I saw the relationship
For what it was
For the first time.
The horrifying realization that
My foundation was an illusion.
I blew a core pillar to smithereens.

Even through a contentious divorce,
I vowed to do everything to get healthy.
I was fully Aware that the Because and the Care
HURT.
I kept telling myself
This is a normal, human emotion.
And that it's okay
To feel.
It's all okay,
To feel this way,
To recognize that this feeling,
Being stressed, uncertain, starting over,
Is difficult.
But the commonality in all of it,
Was my scrawny little body
Kept nudging, "What about me?"
"What about me, Lisa?"

Not until I arrived in Florida,
Did I start to really feel,
And I collapse.
I stay in bed for nearly two weeks,
Just walking Oshie when she needs it.
Everything else can wait.

I reaffirm my vow to take better care of myself.
I start to settle into Florida.
As I start to rebuild the crumbled pillars of
Financial Obligations, Relationships, Good Health
(Yeah, I blew up a few core pillars at the same time)
I haven't yet reprioritized myself in all of this.

In 2019 the illnesses come on:
I get a head cold.
The full-on stuffed head/body aches/nose running like a
river kind.
Then an abscessed tooth
Because I'm a lifelong grinder.
I go to Colorado and get altitude sickness.
I get a urinary tract infection.
Shingles shows up to remind me what pain really is.
Then that little spot that won't heal
Turns out to be skin cancer
On my face.
One after another, little things taken by
Themselves are easy to handle.
But standing back and listening,

I hear my body say,
"This is the result of your inattention.
Now I am making you stop and
Deal with me."

I hear you, body.
I vow once again to take better care of myself.
And this is how things go,
When you use the 7MQ.
Day by day, you make a little progress
And then you feel like you aren't.

The year 2020 was only modestly better:
Pandemic aside, I had a ton to deal with.
Skin cancer removed in January.
Welcome to Mohs surgery.
Some weird GI complaint in February,
For the first time in seven years
I called off work,
Because traveling with a gut complaint
Is just plain stupid.
My gut takes months to start to feel better,
Or so it seems.

Then the teeth.
I get three root canals,
And two caps because
My lifelong grinding is cracking teeth.
Cracking teeth.

One more skin cancer found in October.
That's it, I say to myself.
This is *finally* it.
I need to make more changes
To start putting myself first.

My friend Rolito tells me,
"Lisita, you work too hard.
You have to start taking care of yourself.
You have to do it now, because things will
Get worse when you are older."
Thank you, my older, wiser amigo.

Proactive. I take positive baby steps.
I order organic produce delivery.
I start working out four times a week.
And I take control of my work schedule.

I go back to my Personal Core Foundation,
And I focus my 7MQ on only the things
That are high value.
I turn down the volume on everything else.
And I make sure I am getting enough rest.
I'm in bed by 9:00 p.m. every night.
I put Lisa first.

Each day as I wake up,
I say my prayers and clear any residual energy.
I set my intentions for each day,
And decide what kind of day I'm having.

I take a long soaking bath every single day.
I work out in the morning.
I meditate afterwards.

Then I start to notice, sort of like magic,
The benefit the workouts have
On my body and my emotions.
I start to see how using Aware, Because, and Care
Are paying off.

I am well. I am healthy.
No longer with serial illnesses.
Good health, which was sort of an afterthought
In my six pillars, is now on top.
OMG, I feel so good after I work out.
Then, I am getting into the sixty-degree water in the pool
To cut down on inflammation.
It feels amazing.

I feel deeply.
More importantly,
I recognize that I am feeling deeply.
I really feel less stressed.
And I notice earlier when stress is rising.
I notice and tell my trainer which exercises
Are releasing tension in the spot
Where the chest pain was.
Years after the episode in the ER,
I realize that I hold tension in my chest.

My awareness of what I'm doing and what I'm feeling
Is less subconscious and more conscious.
I notice and react better when I really need to stop working
and eat.
I am more aware of how I feel when I'm hungry.
I am getting better at meal planning,
And making good food choices.

I am feeling stronger,
And what used to be daily gut pain
Is now just occasional discomfort.
Not even pain—just discomfort, and I use my
Digestive Essential Oil on my belly,
And within minutes
I am good.
So, like magic,
I see joy and delight,
In every single day.
It's the persistence that comes from using the 7MQ.
I am strengthening all of the six pillars
Of my Personal Core Foundation.

It takes time to create a habit.
In my case, it's taken two years
Of focused effort to make the changes
To include regular self-care in my routine.
I'm well on my way.

But the point is that,
Change, and significant change in habits,

Is greatly impacted by being aware.
I use the 7MQ to check in,
To monitor how my body,
My mind, and my spirit are doing,
Several times throughout the day.
Because I have a sincere desire
To have good health.
I care about me,
So that I can care about and care for others.
Better.

Taking better care of myself,
Practicing better self-care
Is now an imperative.
I don't want another year of sequential illnesses,
All brought on by inattention to me.
I'm answering that question of
"What about me?"
With me, and only me.
Now, I have time for me.

Don't Be So Hard on Yourself: Practicing Self-Compassion

"Compassion and tolerance are not a sign of weakness, but a sign of strength."

—The Dalai Lama

Sometimes as you use the 7MQ you need to take a deeper dive into Care. Rather than looking outward to what you care about, let's look inward. Let's turn "Why do I care?" and look into your emotional weather to find out what needs your attention.

I'm going to admit it's been really hard lately. Not just for me. I think society is fed up with so much of what's been happening. Ordinary people have been moved to extraordinary measures. When you're in quarantine, you start to pay attention to habits and things that bug you—about yourself. When the distractions of the external world are brought to a minimum, you see things differently. You have time to pay attention. (I can't imagine how people went through the 1918 pandemic without radio or TV. But then, they didn't have to worry about the media sensationalizing everything.)

When you start to use the 7MQ regularly, remember to be curious and neutral. When you start judging yourself for past mistakes, recognize it for what it is. When you notice you are suffering, react with kindness. Some of us use self-judgment as a motivating force, so I'm not going to say self-judgment is totally without merit. But it can be a double-edged sword. On either side, it cuts, and recognize that self-judgment is a longstanding well-grooved habit. The harshness of being tough on yourself, ignoring clear warning signs are where you are cutting yourself (figuratively). Understand that it takes time and steady effort to attempt to heal, over and over. It's time to set the sword down and start learning softer, more nurturing habits. The paradox of strength is knowing when to use self-judgment and when a softer approach will yield better results.

JH Hard, the poet author of *War, Over Easy* says: "There is nothing stronger than a soft soul." I love this quote, and the irony is not lost on me that a guy named Hard is talking about strength through softness. The Seven Mindful Questions are intended to be introspective and may bring up self-criticism, particularly when you realize you don't care about something you are doing. You may recognize that you are getting upset or feeling badly or suffering emotionally in the beginning. Mindfulness is a soft approach that makes you cognizant that, through no direct fault of your own, failure is inevitable—everyone makes mistakes. Being understanding, warm, and kind toward yourself is the type of self-compassion that is rooted in mindfulness.

In the year 2020, life fell short of everyone's ideals (see above poem). The year 2021 hasn't started out much better. We are still quarantined but not alone, as infections and death rates continue without an end in sight. There's a dawning realization that, even with a vaccine, this virus will be around for a long time yet to come. We are all in this together. Acceptance of "what is" can be reinforced, with the kindness of self-compassion. The old habit of self-judgment has worn threadbare and is no longer effective in motivating me to move forward. Maybe you, too, are tired of beating yourself up for your perceived failures. At some point, "piling on" just doesn't work anymore.

The more useful habit of self-compassion has taken its place. I'm going to recommend an "off-book" exercise. You can check your level of self-compassion on Kristin Neff's website: www.self-compassion.org and click on the link Test Your Level of Self-Compassion. I took the test and was pleasantly surprised that I am at 3.4 out of 5 on Self-Kindness. I am absolutely sure that after my ER visit, I would have scored much lower.

Self-compassion means treating yourself with kindness when you fall short of expectations. For most of my adult life, I would wake up early and work before my kids got up, when my brain was fresh. Like *Alice in Wonderland*, I was able to do Six Impossible Things Before Breakfast.

But now, not so much. It's a real struggle to get up and write in the mornings. For most of June and July of 2020, I would wake up at 7:00 a.m., well after the sun was up, which is really weird because I love to watch the summer sun rise—always have. Then, after Oshie time (walking, feeding, brushing, playing), I would sit my butt in my meditation chair and do just that until it was time to go to work at 9:00 a.m. At the end of my morning meditation, I would wrap my arms across my chest, give myself a hug, and say "thank you" for spending time alone in mindfulness meditation. I made a habit of telling myself, "It's all okay" before I'd go about my day.

At the end of the workday, at 5:00 p.m., I would find myself wanting to sleep and have no energy to make dinner. (Did I mention the menu planning thing?) So, I started going to bed super early, like in the early days of living in the beach house in 2017, when I had profound physical exhaustion. This was more mental exhaustion—dragging my butt through my day to get all my work done. There was overwhelm. There was a lot of overwhelm. Using the Seven Mindful Questions showed me that I needed to pay attention to how I was feeling to address the overwhelm with self-care activities, such as pool-time and long, soaking baths. The point is that you need to build in time for self-care. You cannot give from an empty pitcher. Coping with the pandemic has meant scaling way back for me, and I'm okay with that.

Allow yourself to receive, do things that are nurturing, allow yourself to be vulnerable and, above all, go easy on yourself—remembering that everything happens in its own right time. It's all okay, and you are never alone.

Guided Meditation: Self-Compassion and Feelings in Your Body

"Research shows that self-compassion is a powerful way to achieve emotional well-being and contentment in our lives. By giving ourselves unconditional kindness and comfort while embracing the human experience, difficult as it is, we avoid destructive patterns of fear, negativity, and isolation. At the same time, self-compassion fosters positive mind states such as happiness and optimism."

—Kristin Neff

Self-Compassion: The Proven Power of Being Kind to Yourself

Follow these directions for a guided meditation that focuses on your body and feelings in your body. We are going to explore where you may have a feeling stored in your body. If you find it difficult to pay attention to what arises, you can switch your attention to ambient sounds, or another anchor that feels more comfortable. The choice of object to focus on is yours. As thoughts pop into your head, allow them to fade away without attaching to the thought. Recognize that you are thinking and let the thought go. This short meditation is available for download at: https://www.lisanezneski.com/seven-mindful-questions-meditations.

You may find it helpful to use a voice recorder and record your own voice so that you can follow along with the cues. Now let's get ready to meditate.

• • •

I invite you to sit quietly and take a few natural breaths. As you breathe, when it feels natural, close your eyes or cast your eyes downward to limit visual distractions. Take about five natural breaths and feel yourself seated in your chair with your feet flat on the floor. Feel the weight of your body in the chair, in this place and at this time. Take a minute to make yourself as comfortable as possible. Rest your attention in the breath.

As you sit, become aware of how you are feeling, your emotional weather. Are you feeling anxious, fearful, tired, sad, grouchy, or angry? Is your body hungry, angry, lonely, or tired? Are you feeling neutral, negative, or leaning toward the positive end of the scale, toward joy and happiness?

If you are having difficulty feeling your emotional weather, imagine a fuel gauge, with a range of negative feelings on the left near the empty "E," neutral at the top, and positive feelings on the right-hand side of the gauge, near the full "F." Take a second to see where you are on the gauge. Are you on the negative side? Are you on the positive side? Are you feeling neutral with no particular charge at this time? Whatever you are feeling right now, it's all okay. Remember to go back to the breath to refocus your attention—or bodily sensations or ambient sounds, whichever you prefer and is most comfortable.

Allow yourself a full minute to feel whether you are positive, neutral, or negative.

What are you not allowing yourself to feel? Let's look for that unfelt feeling. Take your time and, starting with your feet, gradually scan your body from your feet to the top of your head, looking all the while for a feeling that wants your attention. Find the spot in your body where an unrecognized emotion is sitting and waiting for your attention. Say hello to the feeling: I see you. I am here. You have my full attention. Bring your attention to the center of where the feeling is and use the gauge to assess where you are on the scale.

How are you feeling right now?

Sit with the feeling. Notice the feeling. I invite you to name it: This is anger. This is happiness. This is fear. This is sadness. This is disappointment. Name whatever you are feeling in your own words. Allow the feeling to be. Tell the feeling, "I care about you," and let the feeling show you what needs your attention.

There are times when this meditation uncovers a feeling that is too intense and overwhelming. If the feeling is overwhelming, ask the sensation, what can you be with? If so, back away from the intensity until you can be with what is happening. And then consider: Is there something that the feeling is trying to tell you? What are you not paying attention to? Sit with this feeling for several minutes, backing down the intensity until it is at a

80

level you can tolerate. Feel into what you can be with and see if this feeling has insight for you.

Pay attention to the way you talk to the emotion/yourself. Allow yourself to feel. If at any point the feeling becomes overwhelming or too much, ask yourself "what can I be with or what can I tolerate?", and again, back off some more.

Allow yourself several minutes of quiet reflection to feel and listen to what your body and emotions are trying to tell you. There is nothing to do but listen and breathe.

Rather than fixing this feeling, how can you comfort yourself? Does it feel good to put your hand on your heart? Does it feel better to cross your arms across your chest and give yourself a hug? Does gently rocking back and forth in your chair feel good? Notice what makes you feel more comfortable. Make a note of your most nurturing go-to tendencies.

Now ask the emotion: what do you need to feel better? Other subtle emotions may arise here. Allow those secondary emotions to arise into your awareness. Again, ask the emotions: What do you need to feel better? Better food? Better rest? Focus only on vitals and essentials?

As we begin to bring this meditation to a close, allow yourself to sit in the state of recognition of the emotion and what it is saying. And give yourself permission to feel the feeling. As we would do with a loved one or pet, it's so important to offer ourselves self-compassion, especially when our bodies tell us we're not feeling well. The goal of offering ourselves self-compassion is to acknowledge the feeling, not to change it, not to even make it better, but to allow the feeling to be and to run its course.

Sit quietly until you feel complete and acknowledge the wisdom of mining your emotions for an unmet need. Feel your whole body in space and time and acknowledge your place here, on this chair, in this time, on this planet. Gradually return your attention to your body in your chair, wiggling your toes and fingers, taking a deep breath, stretching, and when you are ready, you may open your eyes.

This meditation may be of a more intense nature, and you may wish to journal about your experiences, noting the nugget you mined and how you can pay better attention to this unmet emotional need.

Now take the nugget of awareness that you mined in this meditation with you.

Well done. This work is not easy.

• • •

QUESTION FOUR:
PAUSE AND BREATHE

The Seven Mindful Questions:

1. What am I doing right now? (Awareness)
2. Why am I doing this? (Because)
3. Why do I care about this? (Care)
4. ***Pause and Breathe.* What else should I be doing? (Pause)**
5. Choose: What is essential? (Choose)
6. What can I do better? (Better)
7. What is the best alternative? (Alternative)

I'm Aware Because I Care.
Pause and Breathe.
Choose the Better Alternative.

Pause

Question Four: ★Pause and Breathe★ "What else should I be doing?"

Pausing and breathing is powerful. When we hit the pause button with this question, we take a breather and review our options. This will help you reset and begin to think more strategically.

As Margaret J. Wheatley says in her blogpost, *Time to Think*: *"Thinking is the place where intelligent actions begin. We pause long enough to look more carefully at a situation, to see more of its character, to think about why it's happening, to notice how it's affecting us and others."*

There is power inherent in the pause. The culmination of the awareness of what we are doing (Aware), the reason behind it (Because), the emotional need it is filling (Care) is to then take intelligent action. The pause that gives you the power in the midpoint of the 7MQ gently brings you back to the present moment, giving you control over the situation.

You have the power. You have the power to control how you react in difficult situations. You have the power to control how you react to people who push your buttons. You have the power of the pause to reframe any situation. You have the power to reset what you are doing—and pivot to higher-value actions.

Pause before you:

- React to the person pushing your buttons
- Send an email. Any email. Yes, any email
- React to that difficult situation, thinking: *How else might I respond?*
- Anytime you sense you are getting tense

In a quote that Steven Covey misattributed to Viktor Frankl, an Austrian neurologist, psychiatrist, and Holocaust survivor, I mean this sentiment: *"Between stimulus and response there is a space. In that space is our power to choose our response. In our response lies our growth and our freedom."* Whether Dr. Frankl said it or not, that space is the pause.

When in conflict, even if the conflict is with yourself, a pause often helps to de-escalate your feelings. When you pause, you begin to listen—to yourself and to others. Every one of us just wants to be seen for who we are. Listening, mindful listening, being present to what our hearts are telling us, or what another person is saying, is a useful skill in building relational muscles. We all want to be acknowledged for who we are and for how we are feeling. Mindful listening fosters the ability to really see, which leads to meaningful insight. The Pause, step four in the Seven Mindful Questions, is strategically placed to allow you to gather your thoughts and think through your options before taking action.

Finding the space between stimulus and response, for me, lies in my daily meditation practice. Even if you don't feel comfortable meditating (yet), you can still take a deep breath, count to ten, and reframe the situation. Pausing allows space for a potentially better solution to enter and allows space for you to see common ground.

There are three helpful techniques that we are going to learn to facilitate the Pause:

1. Grid it out—Get it out of your head in Exercise #6
2. Walk it off—Poem and Guided Meditation
3. Journal it—Write about it

Each of these techniques requires you to slow down and think about ABC ★Pause and Breathe.★ Having options allows the ★Pause and Breathe★ to be the pivotal point of the 7MQ, to help you process your new awareness and keep you focused on what matters.

Grid It Out

Let's move to a task-oriented type of Pause in the Value/Effort Grid. Now that we have paused and taken a breather, bring your attention back to Question #4: "What else should I be doing?" At this point, I'm usually thinking of a dozen other things that I could be doing, but which one *should* I be doing? The use of the word should in the question is intentional. Should is something that ought to happen, a high-value task. Could is just that—it might happen, it could happen, or it might not. Out of everything that could happen, which task is the highest priority, which should happen? A lot of people shy away from the word "should" because it can be a weapon to feel bad about yourself. That is not how we are using it in the 7MQ. We are being very selective with "should," as you will see with the next exercise. You will be able to see what the "shoulds" are as high-value tasks. It is amazing how quickly we can shuffle priorities and recognize the high-value tasks.

Exercise #6: Your High-Value Priorities

Step 1: Take out a sheet of paper and draw a two-square by two-square grid as in the example below. Along the X-axis (the bottom) put the word *Value* and draw an arrow left to right, indicating a higher value moving to the right. Along the Y-axis (the left going upward), put the word *Effort* and draw an arrow bottom to top, indicating higher effort items going up. Label the boxes as below. There are four possible combinations of low- and high-value items combined with low- and high-effort items.

THE VALUE / EFFORT GRID

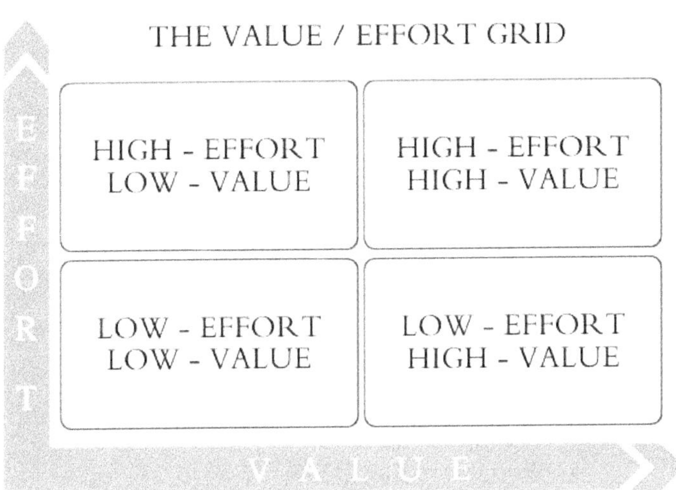

Step 2: Grab a bunch of sticky notes and brainstorm a "could" to-do list, putting one task on each sticky note. Note anything that comes to mind and do not stop to analyze, judge, figure out—just free flow ideas. Any "coulds" and definitely all the "shoulds" each get a sticky note. Set a timer for ten minutes and go! (Any longer than ten minutes and you belong in the Overthinker's Anonymous club. As president, I invite you to attend. We meet next to the Department of Redundancy Department every sixth Tuesday of the month.)

Set that timer for ten minutes. Ready, set, go!

Step 3: Take each sticky note (all your coulds and shoulds) and assign them a priority in a Value/Effort quadrant. Take your time and think through where to put them. For example, High-Value/Low-Effort should (and could) get done with the most ease. The High-

Value/High-Effort are items with the highest importance but may not be finished in one go—and you should work on those. The Low-Value/High-Effort ones are the most taxing with the least reward—but should be done anyway. This is where I put housekeeping activities. The Low-Value/Low-Effort are items that can be skipped entirely and are typically the time wasters.

Reflections on Exercise #6

Here's how mine turned out. Imagine the words in the squares as individual sticky notes:

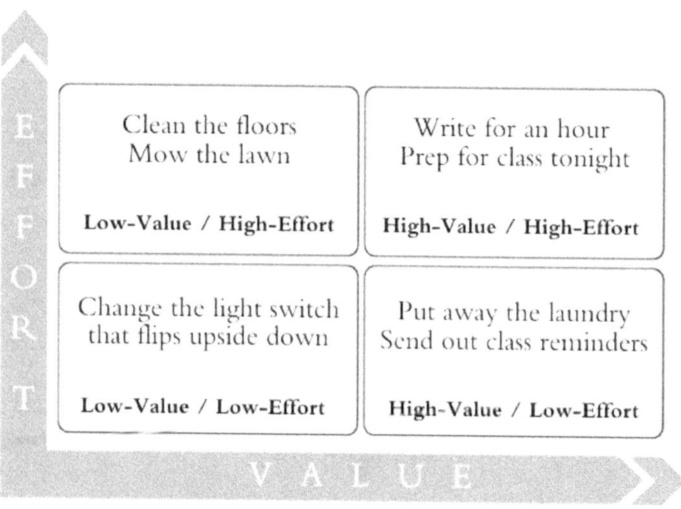

I assigned the laundry/reminders as High-Value/Low-Effort tasks, the easiest and fastest things that should get done today, when I need a mental break. Next, it came down to the two big goals for today in the High-

Value/High-Effort quadrant. I am currently writing this chapter, and I have no time limit at the moment, but I intend to stop by 4:00 p.m. so I can review my notes for an essential oils class tonight. Then, at 5:00 p.m., I'll send out reminders for class, which starts in two hours. As I place the sticky notes in their respective quadrants, I usually get an intuitive hit of a "yes," "maybe," or "no way." When I pay attention to my emotional weather, particularly when I get an intuitive "yes," I know where to place the sticky notes, and I can go to sleep tonight thinking I did a good job.

I dislike cleaning floors, so it went in the Low-Value/High-Effort quadrant. Don't judge me; I just don't like it. It's not like I am unprepared and don't have supplies. I have mops and dust mops and the beloved robotic vacuum named Awesome-O (like Cartman's robot in *South Park*), so there really is no excuse. So, talking myself into it, I say, "Okay, Lisa, when I take that mental break to run upstairs and put the clothes away, I'm going to tack on the extra task that takes all of five minutes to dust mop the upstairs floors, then start the Roomba right before I sit back down to look at the class materials." Did I just plan the Low-Value/High-Effort quadrant? Yes, yes, yes! Yay, me!

And you know what? I will need time to defervesce after teaching tonight, so I bet I can change that light switch out today, too. But, hey, if it doesn't get done, it's a Low-Value/Low-Effort quadrant task for another day.

I've only lived here for nearly two years with a light switch that flips down for "on," I can hack it for a few more days.

That's the secret to the Pause. You can easily see your High-Value/High-Effort tasks and tackle them, and the High-Value/Low-Effort tasks staged next. If you focus on the High-Value tasks, the other things that could get done sometimes actually do.

Results written the next day:

How'd that turn out for you, Lisa? Good news, I got the laundry put away, sent out class reminders, wrote for over an hour, taught a class and dusted the furniture (!) while dust mopping the upstairs floors. Amazing that these were done in my usually most unproductive time of the day, which is 2:00 p.m. to 8:00 p.m. High-Value tasks were done with relative ease and little stress. I forgot it's getting dark earlier so it would not have been advisable to work with electricity in the dark to change the switch out, so the Low-Value/Low-Effort task will have to wait for another time—when the sun is out.

This point in the 7MQ sequence, the Pause and Breathe, "What else could I be doing?" is the inflection point that makes the difference in being able to manage all those thoughts competing for your attention. This part of the sequence is so important in developing the skills for self-regulation and self-management, which are two of the aims of practicing mindfulness. Using the Pause with the grid technique can help you win the day. Getting all that stuff out of your head and onto sticky notes placed on the grid can allow you to focus on those things that matter—High-Value/High-Effort and High-Value/Low-Effort—without being distracted by all the other "coulds and shoulds." When that thought train starts to run in circles on the same track, use the grid technique to get all that stuff out of your head. When all that stuff is out of your head, you can bring your attention to what is happening now. I hope you find this technique as helpful as I do, especially when I'm at a point in the day when I don't know what to do next, I've hopped on the thought train, or I'm on the edge of overwhelm.

By Walking, It Is Solved

I hit the wall.
Meaning, I hit a point of frustration.
Intrusive thoughts interrupt
My concentration.
Accusatory, Self-Critical thoughts.
I messed up. Again.
I think, *I need to take a break.*
So, smack dab in the middle of something
Where I keep making mistakes,
I get up from the desk
And I walk away.
More like I slammed down the mouse with an expletive,
And jumped up, turned, and
Walked without thinking.
I find myself in the bathroom.
Did I really have to pee?
Or did I mindlessly walk
Into the bathroom
On the opposite end of the house from my desk?
Doesn't matter. Just use the bathroom.
I feel the frustration mounting in my whole body.
I call out to Oshie, "Walk time."
And she comes out
From one of her twenty rest spots.
This time from under the bed
And we head downstairs to
Walk the beach.
It's a cold January day.

The wind is thankfully calm.
I can walk and walk without
Being sandblasted by frozen sand
Whipping into my face.
Frozen sand feels like the
Sting of a thousand bees.
Not today.
I feel the cold air as it hits my nostrils.
With every step, I breathe in time.
Inhale—step, step
Exhale—step, step
I hear my breath
Match the cadence of the waves.
Wave In, Retreat, Wave In, Retreat.
Each breath is two steps,
Each wave is two steps.
The ocean is relatively calm.
I walk and gradually start to
Only focus on what surrounds me.
The sun is reflecting and
Sparkling like floating diamonds.
Augenblick.
I look at my phone and 45 minutes
Have passed in an instant.
As I turn back toward home,
I realize that I am
Pissed-off about something
That happened this morning
That had nothing to do with work,
But it carried over.

I had the thought about what to make for dinner.
Once again in January,
I was going to pay more attention to what I eat.
I was going to make the effort to meal plan.
So, this morning,
While I was thinking about what to make,
I found myself self-editing.
I found myself in the middle of
A well-grooved habit of thinking about
What my ex-husband would eat or not eat.
And I pissed myself off royally.
I was a 15 on a scale of 1–10.
I was so angry with myself,
That I was still considering
What he liked to eat,
"As if" he was going to eat it
And was totally subconsciously
CHANGING MY MENU
To his likes and desires.
Even though at this point,
We had been separated
For five months.
I pissed myself off.
Are you serious, Lisa?
You won't make meatloaf because
He doesn't like it.
Fuck You. Fuck Him. Fuck the Meatloaf.
And I keep walking as I replay this in my head.
I start to laugh.
Fuck You. Fuck Him. Fuck the Meatloaf.

I say it out loud to the gulls overhead,
And a big belly laugh from the pit of my stomach
Rolls out like the waves.
Meatloaf.
And I keep walking.
I start running the questions.
What are you doing right now?
I'm walking off my frustrations.
And with each step, I feel the tension
Leaving my body,
Blown off by the good ions from the ocean.
Why are you doing this?
Because I got really frustrated making mistakes.
Why do you Care about this?
OMG, you have no idea how much better
I feel on a good, long walk (with my BFF).
That good, long walk cleared my head
Enough to realize that mistakes were the symptom
Of the inattention to detail.
Thinking of something else entirely
Instead of the task at hand.
(She Pauses to sniff a shell or
The remains of something no longer living.)
I Pause and Breathe.
I look out at the ocean.
I have twenty more minutes of walking
Before I get home.
I have a better understanding
Of what is bugging me.
And with each step,

I breathe and let the frustration go.
Stop being hard on yourself.
Did you notice that you stored that
Royal pissed-offery in your body?
That you subconsciously
Let it simmer on the back burner?
Well, yes, and
That was a mighty
Powerful
Anger.
It's going to keep poking at you until
You deal with it.
Now that I am more aware of it,
I'm walking it off.
St. Augustine was right:
"By walking it is solved."
Solvitur ambulando.
At the Wharton School,
We did an exercise: 15 Minutes
Of Mindful Walking
In between sessions.
I told the professor this saying:
"By walking it is solved."
And he looked up the Latin
And wrote it on the board,
And gave me credit for that
In front of the entire group
All from my company.
It was a moment
I forgot about until

I wrote this.
When that moment of
Supreme frustration hit,
I didn't think about it.
I just got up and walked away.
And I continue walking for an hour and a half—
Until my heart rate,
Which truly increased from frustration,
And my respiration rate
Returned to a normal relaxed breath.
As I hit Beach Access 39
And turn toward home,
I ask myself,
"What else should I be doing?"
It's a short answer.
I'm ready to go back to work and
Finish that calculation.
My head is clearer and
I'm going to go
Make the fucking meatloaf.

Guided Meditation: Walking It Off

One of the ways for beginners to explore mindfulness is by taking a mindful walk. You're walking to walk, not trying to get somewhere. Thich Nhat Hanh explains that mindful walking is done with reverence. It connects our bodies to Mother Earth in a way that is grounding and respectful. A mindful walk is done with one breath per step, and in a way that you begin to take in your surroundings. As you begin to open your awareness to what is happening around you, you begin to notice details you've overlooked before. You notice and appreciate the wonders of life on earth at this time. A mindful walk is a profound way to get in touch with nature.

A mindful walk can also help you walk off problems, as in: "By walking it is solved." St. Augustine most likely had a temperament like mine. Once the level of frustration exceeds the body's ability to tolerate it, you've got to move it. When I am walking to solve a problem, I walk until the problem works itself out of my body. And, as you read, it can take well over an hour. I remember being in Orange County, California and walking on a treadmill, then a track, then a treadmill for four hours, as I realized that it was time to find a new job. The Wharton School included periods of walking in their formal instruction. Most meditation retreats that last over several days include periods of mindful walking. Many people have asked whether running or some other form of physical exercise can be mindful. My firm belief is that any physical exercise that gets you in touch with your body, with your internal weather, can be mindful. And if it exposes you to nature and the elements—bonus. The purpose of the mindful walk is not to get somewhere; the purpose of the mindful walk is to walk, to notice, to be present for the sensations in every step, and to honor the earth on which you stand.

Here is a beginning guided walking meditation. This meditation will require you to prepare by finding a safe place to practice mindful walking. You may start at home or around your home, or on a walking path, or somewhere you can listen to the guided instructions for ten minutes. Finding a space in nature where you can walk and appreciate your surroundings is ideal. When that is not practical, walking inside for a length of ten to fifteen feet is optimal. This is an eyes-open meditation (for obvious reasons).

This short meditation is available for download at: https://www.lisanezneski.com/seven-mindful-questions-meditations. You may find it helpful to use a voice recorder and record your own voice so that you can follow along with the cues.

• • •

Begin by making sure you will be comfortable on this walk. If you are walking inside, make a clear path for ten to fifteen feet that is unobstructed. If you are walking outside, prepare for the elements.

Before you begin to take a step, notice your posture. Gently adjust your body so that your hips and knees are in alignment and your shoulders are over your hips. Set your intention for this walk. As you take your first step, allow your shoulders to drop away from your ears.

Step slowly enough that you begin to pay attention to your surroundings, but not too slowly where you lose your balance. I invite you to allow one full inhale and exhale with each step, or whatever pace feels comfortable to you. You may choose to step with one foot forward, bringing the other foot forward, alongside of the first during the breath cycle so that you feel grounded and balanced. Walk at a slow but comfortable pace that feels right to you.

As you walk, notice the sounds in your environment. You may choose to turn the volume of your headphones down to better hear the sounds around you. Let my voice be softly in the background.

Notice how your breath feels as it enters your body. Is it cool or warm, humid, or dry? Are you timing your breath to your steps? Just simply notice the breath, and if it follows your steps. You may want to release your attention on the breath and breathe naturally.

Notice how your body feels as you walk. Are you moving your arms in time with your steps? Are you stiff or uncomfortable in any way? You may want to roll your shoulders and adjust your posture. As you bring attention

102

to your body, notice any sensations of tightness, tension, or ease. Feel free to make any adjustment in your pace or posture to enhance this walking experience.

Now pay attention to your feet. Notice how it feels to lift a foot off the ground, and how it feels to move the foot through space and then make contact again with the ground. Feel your body shifting your weight from one foot to the next. Notice the sensations in each foot as it contacts the ground. Spend several minutes noticing how your feet make contact with the ground.

It may be helpful to say "step," "step," or "contact," "contact," or "walk," "walk." Naming the motion will continue to bring your focus to the movement.

Now widen your experience to your whole body—the way it feels for your body to walk in this slow and deliberate manner. You have nowhere to go, nowhere to be but right here, walking for walking's sake. Experience your body in this place and in this time.

Begin to open your experience wider, to notice sensations more fully, bringing sights, sounds, smells into your awareness as you make your way. Imagine your body as a ship on the ocean, parting the sea as you go, having the sea close in behind you as you pass, with ripples of energy moving out into the environment, like the wake of a ship. Open to the full awareness of everything around you. As you walk, see if you can be open to everything around you.

What catches your attention? Is there a particular leaf or piece of grass that you haven't noticed before? Is there a tree limb that is an interesting shape? Is there a cloud above that resembles something? Notice the colors of the sky. Notice any sounds of birds or other animals, such as a barking dog. Notice if there are any people, neighbors or children, going about their day. Notice if there are cracks in the sidewalk, being careful to step over tripping hazards.

If you happen on a moment of Augenblick, it's perfectly fine to stop walking to appreciate the sensation of wonderment. Be open to the full experience of this walk at this time.

Continue to walk mindfully, paying attention to your feet as you go. Experience your full environment, as is comfortable for you. Notice your breath, your feet, your body as you move through space, and sounds, sights, and smells in your environment. "Walk, walk." "Step, step." "Breathe, breathe." "Look up," "look around," "walk, walk."

When you are ready to bring this walk to a close, return to your point of origin, slowly turning back in the direction you came from. And, while standing still, take a long, slow deep breath in, and exhale out slowly. Take one more look around to appreciate your surroundings to end this walking meditation.

Well done.

• • •

Mindful Journaling as a Vehicle to the Pause

"Journal writing is a voyage to the interior."
—Christina Baldwin

Let's take a look at a different kind of pause, the pause created by writing something by hand and the slowing of the mind to think as you put your thoughts to paper. Writing and journaling as a mindfulness practice can help get control of racing thoughts, provide an outlet for frustrations, and can help you track your progress over time. In 2010, a group of researchers from Arkansas State University wanted to see if journaling would help college students become more mindful. Their conclusions were that ". . . journal writing served as a preliminary stage to mindfulness and helped students prepare their minds for the subsequent mindfulness exercises." (Khramtsova, Glascock, 2010) It is my hope that you will find that the journaling exercises reinforce the skills in using the 7MQ method and that you will find journaling a doorway to mindfulness. Journaling is a wonderful way to start, especially if you are beginning a meditation practice or want to enhance your current practice.

In healthcare, we have a saying: *Not documented, not done.* If you don't chart the event, who is to say it was ever done? In my professional career as a pharmacist, I spent considerable time studying medication errors and the role of good documentation in error prevention. A mistake in healthcare can be deadly. A nurse can forget to document that a medication was given, leaving the next nurse thinking it still needs to be administered. A patient could easily get twice the intended dose if there isn't documented proof.

Outside of healthcare, we probably aren't aware of all the ways that documentation has crept into our life. Amazon and Netflix have documented your purchases and selections to know your preferences well enough to make suggestions based on your past choices. I have an app on my phone where I chart my food intake. I wear a Fitbit to record my daily steps, and I use an app to record how much sleep I'm getting. (By the way, there are wonderful meditation apps available, too.) Intentionally or unintentionally, your life is being documented, whether you agreed to it or not.

It's taken several years of consistent writing practice to become comfortable with journaling and exploring the inner workings of me. I've had to negotiate with myself to document things of a personal nature. I never kept a diary as a kid. That wasn't a safe activity in my house. I'd squirrel away the odd thought here and there, though. It wasn't until much later in life, when I felt safe enough to explore my thoughts in depth, that I discovered the utility of journaling.

Utility is an understatement. My journals help me go deep into exploring what I think, what I mean, how I organize thoughts, and, most importantly, they create insight into my life. Daily journaling is one of the best ways to find moments of Augenblick. A thought translated to the written word becomes a powerful vehicle for noticing the world around us. It was through my writing practice that the 7MQ took shape and became enlivened.

To get the most from the Seven Mindful Questions, I recommend that you begin documenting your thoughts. Get something—a journal, a tablet, cheap composition book, scrap paper, take notes on your phone, in the 7MQ workbook, whatever—it doesn't really matter. And it doesn't have to be fancy—just something to keep track of your thoughts as we progress through the next phase.

Ideally, two types of journals would facilitate this process. One notebook should be used to handwrite ideas and thoughts in full sentences. The other should be something small that fits in a pocket or purse for when the "odd thought" hits you. And, recently, after a life-long compulsion to physically write on paper, I've been using the Notes app on my smartphone for the odd thoughts— thoughts that are worth capturing that pop into my head. And I use the Notes app on my electronic tablet for longer journaling. Those odd thoughts—those spectacular fleeting moments of Augenblick—have turned into some of my best poems and are fun to review and relive. There are plenty of options. Pick one. Pick two. More importantly, commit to using them daily. And don't wait till you've bought the perfect journal. Perfection is unattainable—just start now.

A mindful journal differs from a diary. You can jot down what you did that day, as long as you add reflections about how you felt. Eventually, it will become an exercise where you begin to document all aspects of your life and your feelings about an event. The purpose of the mindful journaling exercise is to begin to explore what has meaning for you. It was Ralph Waldo Emerson who said, "You become what you think about all day long."

Having a journal handy will help you benefit from the exercises in this book. Having the presence of mind to capture thoughts that pop into your head at odd times will help recall your brilliance. Great ideas happen at odd times. You are brilliant. At odd times. Appreciate yourself.

Also, documenting your life will lead to greater personal accountability. As you begin to move in alignment with your Personal Core Foundation, you'll want to document how far you've come. You can do it. Consistent journaling keeps you honest, moving in the right direction, and focused on the now.

Exercise #7–7MQ Mindful Journaling

Let's use mindful journaling to reflect back on the ABC-Pause of the 7MQ. Even if you are already accustomed to writing as a regular practice, this next exercise dives right into the 7MQ, spending time exploring them on paper. Take the time now to thoughtfully use these questions as a tool to clarify the vision for your life. Soon, you will use the 7MQ in rapid fire, but not yet. The purpose of this exercise is to internalize then externalize (on paper) the first four steps of the Seven Mindful Questions. We are honing the skill in using the 7MQ, so no need to rush.

Instructions

Answer the first question (Aware) below in a list format. Think of the big activities. It's not necessary to include everything, like brushing your teeth (unless, of course, that is a big issue for you, and you feel compelled to include it). Answer the next question (Because) by going back to review your answers and comment next to the item or start a new page—whatever feels most natural. Use the "I am doing this because…." This part of the exercise is similar to the previous exercises.

Answer the next "why" question (Care) by reflecting on your answers to the first two questions. If you think of something to add to #1 (Aware) or #2 (Because) as you are going along, then add it. This should be an iterative process—meaning, with each attempt, you get closer to a better answer.

When you feel complete with answers to questions ABC, complete the ★Pause and Breathe.★

Exercise #7—Mindful Journaling

Get out your paper journal and spend at least twenty minutes answering the following questions of the Seven Mindful Questions:

1. **What am I doing today?** (Aware) List everything you are doing, and everything you plan to do, as completely as possible. Take your time and list everything that is significant to you, even if you know you might not get to it today.

2. **Why am I doing this at all?** (Because) Reflect on each activity and document your Because. Don't overthink it. Write what comes to mind first. I am doing this because…

(Tip #1: I use a different color ink to answer this question, right next to the first answer.)

(Tip #2: If you answer the Because authentically, it's natural and easy to move into C: Why I Care.)

3. **Why do I care about this?** (Care) Take the next step "down the stairs" and think about the role each activity plays in your life. What physical or emotional need is this action fulfilling? What need are you avoiding by considering this action? Feel into it and write about it.

(Tip #3: Write until you feel complete, with no more to say on the subject.)

4. *Pause and Breathe.* What else should I be doing? Now take a handful of sticky notes and create a big 2x2 grid with Value on the X-axis and Effort on the Y-axis. Then plot out which tasks fit into which quadrant according to how much you value them and how difficult it might be to get them done. Map out every single task. Don't take shortcuts by eliminating something that you know won't get done today. In other words, don't self-edit. Assign every single task to a quadrant based on Effort and Value. Then, stand back and reflect. Pause and Breathe again. Move things around until you are satisfied that they have the right Value/Effort for now.

Reflections on Exercise #7

Thinking about what you're doing, feeling into it, and understanding "why" you're doing it is the first step in the Seven Mindful Questions to examining and documenting your life. Understanding why something is important to you adds an evaluative element to the process. If you're like me, when you begin to reflect on what you're doing and why, you start to think of other items to add to your to-do list.

As I was listing my "Because" in a different color ink, I added items to the "What am I doing today?" as they popped into my head. By documenting, you can start to see patterns and trends, and your values, your intentions, and your actions are reflected in the list. By documenting—the physical act of writing it down—awareness develops that leads to a more conscious desire to strategically use your time consistent with your Personal Core Foundation.

Over time, you'll naturally quit wasting time on filler activities and procrastinating to avoid more important tasks. When you see the Low-Value/Low-Effort tasks mapped out, it is much easier to let them go. Using the first four questions of the 7MQ in sequence is the starting point of self-knowledge, it establishes the framework for ongoing self-negotiation, and it's four steps inward to deeper reflection. This initial effort with the first four questions sets the stage for everyday mindfulness by teaching you what's worth paying attention to in your life.

Once you have mapped your tasks in the High-Value/Low-Effort and the High-Value/High-Effort quadrants, you are ready to pivot and come back up the stairs.

QUESTION FIVE:
CHOOSE

The Seven Mindful Questions:

1. What am I doing right now? (Awareness)
2. Why am I doing this? (Because)
3. Why do I care about this? (Care)
4. *Pause and Breathe.* What else should I be doing? (Pause)
5. **Choose: What is essential? (Choose)**
6. What can I do better? (Better)
7. What is the best alternative? (Alternative)

I'm Aware Because I Care.
Pause and Breathe.
Choose the Better Alternative.

Choose

Question Five: "Choose: Which of these are essential?"
Making choices is directly influenced by the same
elements that influence whether you Care about
something. They lead you to Choose where to put your
energy. It's fairly easy to make the value-based choices as
you reflect on your Value/Effort grid. The Value grid
guides you to a natural choice that is aligned with your
Personal Core Foundation. It works very well in the
simple example I gave above when I only had one or two
priorities for the day.

That's not always the case. What happens when you
complete the Pause and the High-Value/High-Effort
quadrant has several really important things? What
happens when you have multiple competing priorities and
you have competing demands for your time? That's when
"essential" comes into play. Don't think of essential as the
bare minimum. It's quite the contrary. Essential items are
necessary and one step above vital biologic imperatives.
Essential items fill a need and often have an emotional
tone. One example of an essential choice is not scheduling
a work meeting at the time your child needs to be on

Zoom for school. If your child needs your supervision, you plan around that.

An essential choice is typically in the High-Value quadrants. So, using that as a starting point, let's say you have five things in the High-Value/High-Effort quadrant:

1. Writing a lecture (something that takes sustained focus)
2. Preparing for a high-stakes client meeting (something that has future implications)
3. Assisting the kids with schoolwork, homework, or online school (something that is a parental responsibility)
4. Taking an elderly family member to the doctor (something that has family responsibility)
5. Taking the car to the shop to fix that funny noise (something that has broader implications on your ability to function)

Certainly, these are important tasks, and you care about all of them. There is a lot on your plate here. It is important to recognize that pulling your focus in multiple directions simultaneously causes stress. The antidote for that stress is to be present in the moment. If you look at the five choices I listed, it comes down to being present for your commitments, your customers, your kids, your family, and yourself. In each of those instances, the person on the receiving end of your attention (or inattention) knows and feels when you are bringing your whole self to the encounter. Being present in the moment means acknowledging that there are other commitments and priorities but, for this moment, "you are here." When you are present and attentive, your ability to perform brings your best self.

I can't tell you which of the five High-Value tasks to do first. I'll leave that to your capable hands, and your ability to block out time for scheduled appointments and school hours. The High-Value/Low-Effort items might sneak in when you need a mental break from the High-Value/High-Effort items, and if that works for you, great.

Looking back at the list of High-Value items, two items have a specific time, and three are somewhat flexible. For me, if the car is still drivable, I would put that off. When the kids are fed and settled into Zoom, I would outline the most important points of my high-stakes client meeting. Being present in the client meeting means being able to connect on a human level, making sure that I attempt to see their issues from their point of view.

Never underestimate the power of eye-contact. When you look someone in the eye, you show them that nothing else in the world is as important as this interaction. That's why it's preferable to be on camera these days, over phone calls. You can be present and make eye contact. (I just have to be careful not to roll my eyes. LOL.) That goes for everything. Being present, making eye contact, being engaged in the interaction without external distraction is the key to mindfulness in business and in life.

Here's a tip, and I can't stress this enough: if two tasks occur at the exact same time, you cannot be two places at once, so move one of them. Grandma needs your full attention, so move that appointment to a time when you can be fully present. I promise this will make a stressful responsibility easier.

I use an online calendar that is part of work email for work appointments, a paper calendar for long-range personal planning, and the calendar on my phone for personal appointments and engagements. So, phone in hand and calendar up on the screen, I look at how much time it will take to do something, block off the time-sensitive material, and work around the other priorities.

Did you notice I didn't put anything at all to do with health, nutrition, or fitness on my grid? These are personal priorities, but there are days I take shortcuts and days when I shuffle things around because I must—I really mean the imperative *must*—take better care of myself. And maybe try out a new meatloaf recipe.

Bad Choices—Noting Your Patterns

"Find your pattern. Find your lesson."
—Maria Cristina McDonald

The sum of your life can be described as the sum of the moment-to-moment choices you make. The goal of 7MQ is to help you make better moment-to-moment choices. When you start to see recurring themes, recognizing where you could have made a better choice, you start to see the freedom in making better choices. Choices equal change. This chapter on Choosing is about recognizing mistakes and making clear and painful observations early on to make a course correction. To effectively use the Seven Mindful Questions as a change management tool, it's important to recognize: what old habits need to change, where you get stuck, and what no longer serves you. Recognizing that something needs to change is the first step to changing it. Here's how to recognize your patterns so you can begin to work on them.

Broken Record

Back in the vinyl music album days, if a record got scratched, it would get stuck on the same section of a song, playing it over and over—a broken record. Take a step backward and imagine that you are looking at your thoughts and actions through the continuum of your life. For most of us, there are recurring themes—the themes of the stories that repeat, for example. The players change, the circumstances change, but the storyline is the same. Like a broken record, the same issues keep playing over and over. I'm no different. In fact, my most painful lessons have revolved around repeated financial mistakes.

I left out some details of how I ended up living in an RV in an industrial park in North Carolina. Suffice it to say, I had terminal financial issues. I kept making financial mistakes until I consciously learned the lesson. In 2014, I had to sell my house in Pittsburgh to get out of IRS debt. Selling the house to deal with financial hardship was not the first time that money trouble reared its ugly head.

Sometime in the late 1990s, my then-husband got a second mortgage on our house to have cash for his business. "Two Self-Employed Entrepreneurs Create Cash Tides. Film at Eleven" That was our headline. We either had a lot of money, or we had very little money. In retrospect, getting the second mortgage was one of the top five worst decisions in my past. Hindsight is always 20/20. My job lent itself to being the steadier income in the family. However, this loan quickly became more than we could handle, and my husband's business eventually closed in 2002. Shortly afterward, things got really tight.

We got behind on the second mortgage loan and—even though we made all the payments (late) and the bank recorded them—they moved the loan into default status. At the time, we had teenagers, and foreclosure meant homelessness. Way before the crash of 2008, the bank was betting on our failure to not make payments on time—and they were coming after our home.

Long story short, a national mortgage chain saw that we'd made all the payments and refinanced the debt. Yikes, that was a horrible experience.

If you thought that was enough to scare us into better financial management, you thought wrong. Either from focusing on the wrong fixes, fear, or a combination of both, this lesson took a few more years of hardship to learn, including my own lesson as a silent enabler.

You are doomed to repeat mistakes until you learn the lesson you are presented with and move on. I shared this issue with you to prove that no matter what you're going through, you can make better choices. Once you recognize a pattern, you can name it and learn from it. Once you know better, you really can do better. You need not have ended up in the ER with a steadily declining heart rate, or in a near-epic financial collapse. Everyone experiences "stuff" and "issues." No matter what you call it, you can face those issues and move beyond them. You move beyond them by going through them.

Some of my mindfulness meditation teachers say, "Let it pass through you." They mean an emotion, a circumstance. This means you accept it, acknowledge it, face it, and then you allow it to move on, beyond you. If you are ready to upgrade your life, you can and will let it go without attaching to it. This is a foundational step to self-knowledge: Recognize and learn from the repeating patterns in your life so you can move beyond them. But be ready because the change is going to hurt.

"The best way out is through."

—Robert Frost

Exercise #8—Pattern Recognition

"Insanity is doing the same thing over and over again and expecting different results."

—Albert Einstein

An important step to changing your life is to recognize the similarities in the painful experiences. The purpose of this exercise is to help you detect patterns and start the process of learning the lesson presented.

Think back over your last couple of painful episodes. You may want to review your journal to identify commonalities and patterns. This exercise can dredge up some powerful emotions, and that is the purpose, too. You won't feel great about the recurring patterns, but you'll have a clear awareness of what they are. I still cringe when I read about the bank experience. (I actually have a credit score in the *very good* range these days, and I'll be out of the divorce debt in 2021. Yay, me!)

Recognition of what needs to change is deeper than awareness. Recognition is that painful and obvious conclusion that the future, as it currently stands, is totally untenable, unacceptable, and not sustainable. Recognition might just force you to make lasting change. Or recognition might be fraught with so much emotion that you need to process all of that before the change can be lasting. This is one of the major tenets of mindfulness—to become aware of the emotional pain that needs to be addressed. Wherever you are in the process, at whatever stage, it's important to acknowledge yourself and accept the situation without judgment or blame. Even if you created all these problems, it's not helpful to hold on to that guilt or blame. Do something different the next time you're presented with a similar issue. Prove that you can do things differently. Prove that you learned the lesson.

If, like me, you're good at blocking out painful events, you might want to create a timeline of these events to help you complete this exercise. By reflecting, you begin to see the patterns.

Instructions

There are four sequential questions in this next exercise that we will use to build on for subsequent exercises. Each will require thought and reflection. This exercise is not timed, so take it slow. That way, you can process the emotions that arise. You may want to start the exercise, then let your subconscious work on it for a while and come back for several iterations over the next few days.

Exercise #8 Pattern Recognition

Get out your journal and answer this question:

1. Where have I repeated something more than once in my life?

Sit with the theme. Make a list of the things that pop into your head. Replay one or two of the episodes over in your mind and make some notes. As a starter, do an inventory using these prompts:

- Relationships
- Parenting
- Finances
- Job
- Other family concerns
- Friendships that tanked
- Business decisions
- Any other area that is a recurring problem

2. For this not to repeat, what needs to change?
   - What is the pattern?

3. How do I feel about the recurring themes?
   - What emotion does each of the episodes bring up?
   - Sit with the emotion for a while.
   - See where it lives in your body. Where do you feel it?

4. What am I to learn here?
   - What is the lesson in my pattern?

Reflections on Exercise #8

There's no doubt that recurring themes in your life exist; they're part of life. Clarity can expose unresolved issues, open old wounds, and generally dredge up things you'd like to forget. Be kind to yourself. We all make mistakes. You can go back to the self-compassion meditation if this has brought up some uncomfortable feelings. I've made big mistakes. My mistakes are embarrassing and, frankly, I'm amazed it took me so long to recognize the patterns. They were right there in my face daily. However, when you're neck-deep in issues, pattern recognition is the last thing on your mind.

Once you know your recurring theme, you can stop behaving unconsciously and bring a mindful awareness to the role the theme plays in your life. You may not be able to make an abrupt discontinuation of the behaviors, and it may take time to make a course correction. Those patterns you have "as if" something is still there but now gone can be well entrenched. That's okay. You didn't get to this place overnight, so be kind to yourself as you mindfully and consciously change your behavior.

You may also pleasantly discover that you have some patterns that are good for you. You may have made good choices that have served you well. Pattern recognition can reveal strengths as well as weaknesses, so play to your strengths and work on your weaknesses.

Continue to ask yourself well-crafted questions to gain more self-knowledge. Understanding yourself, particularly how you think, act, and behave, is a lifelong pursuit. Once you start using the practice of asking yourself open-ended questions and documenting in your mindful journal, you begin to make connections. The connections lead to the recognition of recurring themes. Documenting helps you determine how many times the same theme has played out in your life, and it helps you examine how you feel about it. When you begin to see the themes as an impetus for change, you begin to learn the lesson presented. You can begin to manage self-change. Otherwise, you find yourself living the same situation over and over. It's time to wake up to the realization that you write your own story. You write your own story, and you can change the ending.

QUESTION SIX:
SETTER

The Seven Mindful Questions:

1. What am I doing right now? (Awareness)
2. Why am I doing this? (Because)
3. Why do I care about this? (Care)
4. ⋆Pause and Breathe.⋆ What else should I be doing? (Pause)
5. Choose: What is essential? (Choose)
6. **What can I do better? (Better)**
7. What is the best alternative? (Alternative)

I'm Aware Because I Care.
⋆Pause and Breathe.⋆
Choose the Better Alternative.

Better

Question Six: "What can I do better?"

"Beyond living and dreaming there is something more important: Waking up."

—Antonio Machado

Even though you recognize your patterns, it still may not be enough to spark change. For a change to occur, you must feel it, and the feeling has to light a fire within you. Change is not easy, but deliberate change is empowering. It just feels like hell going through it. Nothing is different until you are.

Question Six: "What can I do better?" should evoke an emotional response. In his book *Awaken the Giant Within*, Tony Robbins describes the great motivators of change as emotional states. Basically, you want it badly enough to do something about it. He further labels them as either "moving toward" or "moving away" values. What drives us to change are the positive feelings that propel us forward or the powerful negative feelings that make us realize we never want to feel that way again.

As for the motivation brought on by negative thoughts, the emotions that accompany a wake-up call can lead to some entirely self-critical thoughts. However, there are times when the kindest thing you can do is KYOA (kick your own ass), but don't be too hard on yourself. This is a double-edged sword: self-judgment meets self-improvement. You can either cut through what is holding you back, or you can allow the sword to turn inward with those self-critical thoughts that hurt all over again. Choose the former and let go of the negative thoughts. Not clinging to negative thoughts is a challenge addressed in mindfulness meditation. Letting go of thoughts, especially negative thoughts, is part of the deepening process of mindfulness. If you hold yourself in great self-compassion, recognizing that we all make mistakes and the common humanity in making mistakes, using some of your default self-nurturing techniques and being willing to forgive yourself, you can move beyond repeating patterns, bad choices, and mistakes.

Sometimes the kindest and most mindful thing you can do is to label that negative emotion, for example: "This is anger." "This is disgust." "This is disappointment." Naming takes the negative charge off the emotion. There really is something magical about naming a negative emotion. It makes it less abstract. It becomes an "I see you" moment. When you recognize your patterns, the emotional jolt can motivate you to make better decisions and rewrite your story. You can liberate yourself from unconscious repeating patterns.

Make the choices that move you in alignment with your Personal Core Foundation and toward your life goals.

I often think to myself: Why do people settle for limited opportunities? Why don't they see what they are capable of becoming? I would see this in my employees when I was in Hospital Administration. Those who didn't believe in themselves struggled. Those who were seeking an opportunity flourished. (I'm thinking of you, Sheila, Donna, Dawn, Cindy.) I spent years cheering for those who didn't believe in themselves—until I learned that what I believed or desired for those around me who struggled didn't matter. What matters is what I believe about myself and my abilities. We need to do the work ourselves.

Change is hard. Sometimes, it seems impossible. Not everyone can make the tough decisions. Living in the "familiar groove" has the inertia brought on by comfort. No judgment here. When you are ready, better choices can be made. Making better choices takes you way out of your comfort zone. When you realize aspects of your life must change in order to begin to live *on purpose and in alignment* with your Personal Core Foundation, you do as Tony Robbins says: *"Awaken the Giant."* You may have once enjoyed those habits, but you begin to see that you have outgrown them, moved beyond them, or the purpose no longer exists. The vantage point of something better when you step upward and out of the habit is the reward for taking the brave step to change.

Guided Meditation: Self-Compassion and Letting Go

This meditation focuses on letting go of difficult feelings and self-critical thoughts. As thoughts pop into your head, allow them to fade away without attaching to them. Recognize that we all experience difficulty, and you can be kind to yourself. We will start with a short grounding exercise to assist with letting go and then shift to examine a situation where you have experienced difficulty. Pick a situation that has a mild to moderate level of difficulty. The most difficult situation may be too intense for this first meditation. This short meditation is available for download at: https://www.lisanezneski.com/seven-mindful-questions-meditations. You may find it helpful to use a voice recorder and record your own voice so that you can follow along with the cues. Now let's get ready to meditate.

• • •

Begin by finding a comfortable position in your chair, resting your feet flat on the floor and your back against the chair. Take a full deep breath and blow out your exhalation with an audible sigh. Take another deep breath and sigh. Repeat one more deep breath and sigh. Now, return your breathing to normal. When you are ready, I invite you to close your eyes, or cast them downward to limit visual distraction.

Next, we will practice grounding to help you with letting go. You can choose to use the image of tree roots, a beam of light, or a waterfall emanating from your hips and dropping downward to connect you with the earth. As you sit in your chair, imagine your hips sprouting roots that go downward through the chair, through the floor, through the foundation of the building, down into the earth below, down through the layers of dirt and rock and heat and pressure, and finally arriving at the center of the earth. As you arrive at the center of the earth, you will see a hook with your name on it. Attach your grounding to the hook and give it a tug to make sure it's secure. Breathe.

Slowly bring your attention back upward to your body.

As you return your focus back to the chair, feel your solid connection to Mother Earth through your grounding. You can use this grounding anytime you feel a bit off-center, especially when you are feeling into a difficult situation or have recognized you made a mistake. Feel the sensation of your body against the chair.

Allow yourself a full minute to feel the sensations of the body.

Keep your focus on the body as an anchor or use breath or ambient sounds as your anchor. If your mind wanders and thoughts begin to drift, return your focus to sensations in your body. It may be helpful to name the thoughts or feelings that arise. "This is thinking, thinking." Or, "this is frustration." Putting a name to the sensation or thought can reduce the emotional charge.

Now, I invite you to bring to mind a recurring pattern or a mistake or situation that's difficult to face. Bring to mind what happened or what you think might have happened. Breathe. Feel the shift in your bodily sensations as you bring this situation to mind. As you hold this situation in your mind, I invite you to acknowledge that this situation is difficult. I invite you to notice what is happening in your body and how you are feeling as you hold this situation. You might be feeling afraid or uncomfortable. Use the skill of naming to gently investigate how this situation is impacting you. Notice the location of sensations in your body as you investigate this situation.

Next, recognize that difficulty is part of life. Remind yourself that difficulties happen to every person on the planet and that difficulties are part of our common humanity. Like all things, difficulties arise, shift, and pass away. Feel your connection to the earth and to everyone who has experienced difficulty. What would you say to someone dear who is experiencing this same difficulty? What words of comfort might make you feel comfortable right now? Say, "It's okay." Now, place a hand on your heart, or rock yourself, with your arms across your chest. Treat yourself as you would someone dear who's experiencing the very same situation. Breathe.

134

Now with each cycle of breath, offer words of comfort. Inhale, It's okay. Exhale, Let go. Inhale, I'm here for you. Exhale, Let go. Inhale, You aren't alone in this. Exhale, Let go. As you let go, drop any sensations and excess emotions down the grounding link for Mother Earth to recycle. Continue to breathe normally, noting what feels comforting on the inhale and dropping any sensation down the grounding link on the exhale.

Allow yourself one to two minutes to let go.

When you feel complete, acknowledge that this difficulty will pass and that you will get through it. Offer words of kindness to yourself as we start to bring this meditation to a close: "May I be happy. May I be healthy. May I stay grounded. May I be kind to myself in this moment." Repeat these words of kindness to yourself: "May I be happy. May I be healthy. May I stay grounded. May I be kind to myself in this moment."

Finish this meditation with a long, slow inhalation and an audible sigh on exhalation. And, one more deep breath in, and release with a sigh. Slowly bring your attention back to the room and to your chair by wiggling your fingers or toes and, when you're ready, you may open your eyes.

Thank yourself for taking time to work through this difficulty and the process of letting go.

• • •

"I need new friends."
That one time I recognized a pattern
and started making better choices.

November 30, 2014 was a typical Monday with one exception—it was my birthday. I started the day having breakfast with my son and his wife after they worked a night shift at the hospital. I was driving to Alexandria, Virginia, for a work meeting, so it was nice to celebrate with family early. My son is always so thoughtful, and that day was no exception.

At that time, I was the sounding board for my sister, my sister-in-law, and a couple of friends who called constantly. I am always available, and I make a point to listen and be there for them. So, on this day, during the six-hour drive, I was anticipating that my friends would reach out and say, "Happy birthday," and I was ready.

I was thinking about how I'd recently gone through several rounds of intense discussions with my friends about their lives when this thought suddenly occurred: *Who is there for me?*

No one. Remembered. My birthday.

I got two late-night texts from my sister and sister-in-law, so they technically did remember, but I was already asleep. And I went to bed that night thinking: *I need new friends.* This was my Tony Robbins "moving away" moment. Over the next year, I just happened to move 500 miles away. It took moving to North Carolina to really wake-up and make all the hard changes I needed to find new friends. I did it, but one could say I had some assistance when I decided to Choose differently. (Thank you, Universe.) Then I moved yet another 500 miles south to Florida to start my life over. Yay, me!

Like in the forgotten birthday story, recognition can be sudden, painful, and motivating. Insight into a pattern that was no longer serving me was inevitable. And the kick in the pants that I needed to change was the pain of not being remembered—that I kept attracting people into my life that were takers, not givers. This insight led to a wake-up moment. I needed friends who were on a more equal footing of give and take. In 2021, I am still working on this issue. The theme of 2021 is "reciprocal." Stay tuned to see how this turns out.

It was time to let go of what was no longer serving me.

And now, you all know my birthdate—I expect a call or text.

Move to North Carolina—Change Your Life

Driving near Savannah, it hit me.
It was North Carolina.
I went through big life changes in North Carolina.
I got approval for a mortgage in 1992.
I quit a job in 2005.
I got hired for a job in 2005.
I interviewed for my current job.
There were more things, like a Deloitte interview.
All when I was in North Carolina.
It hit me that this
Big change
Had to happen
When I was in North Carolina.
It never would have happened
If I had been living anywhere else.
I don't know what it is
About North Carolina.
But if you want to
Throw your life into
Utter upheaval,
Move to North Carolina.
But batten down the hatches
And close the storm shutters;
You are in for an emotional hurricane.

From *Grounded in Chaos*. First published May 2020.

Exercise #9—"What can I do better?"

You have identified patterns that are not worth repeating. Now you can begin to Choose differently. You've made it to the next step: "What can I do better?"

Bringing the problem into conscious awareness and recognition is often enough to fix it. However, in my experience, we learn those lessons incrementally. Meaning, we partially fix an issue without really facing it head-on.

Instructions

Take a few minutes to go back and look at your answers from Exercise #8. If you mined a nugget of pattern recognition worth working on, continue to work with that nugget in this exercise. Re-reading your previous answers and feeling into them may help you gain clarity into what is no longer serving you and help answer Question Six: "What can I do better?" (To clarify: You have the choice in this exercise to work with your existing answers from Exercise #8 or start fresh.) We all have more than one recurring pattern, so if you are starting fresh, be sure to work through all questions below. Identifying your wake-up call is important when laying the groundwork for deciding to make changes in your life. If you're picking up where you left off in Exercise #8, start with #5 below.

Exercise #9—"What can I do better?"

Get out your journal and answer this question:

1. Where have I repeated something more than
    once in my life?

Sit with the theme. Make a list of the things that pop
into your head. Replay one or two of the episodes over in
your mind and make some notes. As a starter, do an
inventory:

- Relationships
- Parenting
- Finances
- Job
- Other Family Concerns
- Friendships that tanked
- Business decisions
- Any other area that is a recurring problem

2. What needs to change?
    - What is the pattern?

3. How do I feel about the recurring themes?
    - As I begin to replay the episode, what
      emotions arise?
    - Allow yourself to really feel the emotion and
      begin to label it. Example: "This is anger."
      "This is disgust." "This is disappointment."
    - Sit with the emotion for a while.

- See where it lives in your body. Where do I feel it?

4. What am I to learn here?
   - Life is a series of lessons. There are greater philosophical principles at work here, but if you can finally learn a lesson, you can move on.
   - What is the lesson in my pattern?
     (Pick up with answers from Exercise #8 here)

5. Why do I think I have repeated a theme?
   - What is yet unlearned?

6. Where or what can I do better?
   - How do I feel about the theme?
   - Where does the feeling sit in my body?
   - Did I get the twinge in my gut?
   - Do I have a physical sensation like a headache?
   - Do I feel weary overall?
   - Can I make use of the feeling and the physical sensation as a course correction to stop the repeating pattern?

Reflections on Exercise #9

This exercise is designed to evoke emotions, so if you're feeling lousy, I'm sorry—truly. However, you and I both know that you had to arrive at this point: the point of no return. The issue is no longer tolerable, and you are ready to move beyond it. You will begin to feel better soon, I promise.

This is the promise of the Seven Mindful Questions: When you begin to use the process of asking the questions in sequence, you will receive instant feedback on whether you are repeating a pattern and, if so, how to make a course correction to work toward a meaningful goal. These answers are extremely helpful self-checks: Are you remaining true to your Personal Core Foundation? Don't spend too much time feeling bad about your choices. Focus, instead, on what you have learned and what you can do better. Note how far you have come already.

Exercise #10—Willingness to Change

There is a study in the change management literature from the 1990s that looked at people who quit smoking. The conclusion of the study was that people quit smoking when they're ready for change—you've got to want it. Only you can decide when you're ready, and what you want versus what you're willing to live with. As we look back at the ABC-Pause-CBA process, to make overarching lasting changes, the recognition of where you could do better and the hard step of making that change for a better alternative are baked into the 7MQ process. We did some heavy lifting to clarify your Personal Core Foundation and determine your unmet needs, and we looked at repeating patterns in your life all to come to this point to determine your willingness to change.

Instructions

In Exercises #8 and #9, you identified unhealthy repeating patterns. You may want to review your answers to those exercises before starting. We are building on the answers from Exercise #8 and #9, to answer the deeply personal question that gives you the courage to address your issue head-on.

What is your pattern? Why should you change it? What opportunity for growth is presented? Are you ready to address it? *"Do I even understand the lesson?"* You know you need to change. The voice in your head is saying "stop." But you may not have a clue how to change. Don't worry about that; that's not what the question is asking. The actual process of making the change comes later. Right now, we are focused on finally learning the lesson presented in the pattern. Just go deep and ruminate to understand the lesson. After each answer to "Do I understand the lesson?" ask, "Is that all I am to understand?"

Keep going until you feel complete.

Exercise #10—Willingess to Change: Lessons Learned

Get out your journal and answer this question:

1. Where have I repeated something more than once in my life?
   - Sit with the theme. Replay one or two of the episodes over in your mind.

2. How do I feel about the recurring themes?
   - What emotion does each of the episodes bring up?
   - Sit with the emotion for a while.

3. What am I to learn here?
   - Why do I think I have repeated a theme?
   - What is yet unlearned?

4. What is my wake-up call?
   - How do I feel about the pattern?
   - Did I get the twinge in my gut or a bit of discomfort somewhere in my body?
   - Is my body telling me something?

5. Do I understand the lesson the recurring theme is trying to teach me?
   - Go deep. After each answer, ask: Is that all I am to understand?
   - Is there anything else I should know?
   - Keep asking until you feel complete.

Reflections on Exercise #10

You don't need to know how to change the issue you have identified just yet. As you use the 7MQ in your everyday life, you will start to get clarity on what the action steps are to keep you in alignment with your Personal Core Foundation. A small change in the questions you ask yourself will lead to exponential changes in the direction of your life.

Change can't happen all at once. You are creating the discipline to check in with yourself on a moment-to-moment basis with the Seven Mindful Questions. The opportunities to make changes will present themselves when you finally deeply understand your patterns. A deep understanding doesn't mean you will immediately make the change. I guarantee you will repeat a minor portion of the pattern with full awareness while it's happening. However, you won't keep repeating the big life-altering mistakes of the past. This time, the repeat won't be nearly as painful. The willingness to change will present you with alternatives. These alternatives will be even better than you imagined because you are working hard to live in alignment with what matters to you.

Let's take that final step up to Alternatives.

QUESTION SEVEN: ALTERNATIVES

The Seven Mindful Questions:

1. What am I doing right now? (Awareness)
2. Why am I doing this? (Because)
3. Why do I care about this? (Care)
4. ★Pause and Breathe.★ What else should I be doing? (Pause)
5. Choose: What is essential? (Choose)
6. What can I do better? (Better)
7. **What is the best alternative? (Alternative)**

I'm Aware Because I Care.
★Pause and Breathe.★
Choose the Better Alternative.

Alternatives

Question Seven: "What is the best alternative?"
"What is the best alternative?" This question brings the 7MQ to a natural conclusion. You begin to reap the reward of all the work you have done with the six previous questions. The "I'm Aware Because I Care" is the wake-up call. The "Pause/Breathe" aligns you with your Personal Core Foundation. The "I Choose Better" shows patterns and gently nudges you to take that hard look at what needs to change. Now we have reached the step where the execution of the Alternatives will confirm that you are living true to your Personal Core Foundation.

Within each choice, and the intention to do better, comes infinite possibilities. As you take that step up to the top of the stairs, look up and see the vastness of the sky. Appreciate it. This is your "I can do anything" moment, but there is such a thing as too many choices. Infinity is much too large for practicality, and there are good ways to meter out the execution of the choices you make. Question Seven helps you do just that by examining the possibilities from all angles.

There is a negotiation technique that is known as the best alternative to a negotiated agreement (BATNA). When agreement can't be reached, BATNA is a useful negotiation technique that examines the relative merit of alternatives and reveals the outcome that matters most. In the application of the 7MQ, choosing a better alternative is a type of negotiation with yourself. As you work through the process, what you are willing to live with and what matters most become clearer.

You can make better choices—I know you can—but where the rubber meets the road is in the execution of those choices. Up to this point, the better choice is an intention. We all know the saying about the road to hell is paved with good intentions. Let's make the alternatives achievable.

The real benefit of 7MQ is using them when the personal stakes are high, and the implications of the decision will be long-lasting or "keep you up all night" heavy. Examining and evaluating Alternatives is a discipline that involves looking at each choice from every vantage point. Bringing to mind all six pillars of your Personal Core Foundation will provide that visibility. What matters most to you is a complex system with the interplay among each pillar of your foundation, which is not mutually exclusive. As a reminder, here are the major pillars of the Personal Core Foundation:

- Relationships—All the people in your life
- Homelife—Where and how you are living
- Work Life—All the aspects of your work life that are fulfilling
- Financial Obligations—How you are able to meet your responsibilities
- Spiritual Life—How you connect with your Higher Power
- Health—Your ability to maintain good health

"What is the best alternative?" Question Seven encourages you to consider how each Alternative impacts the individual six pillars to show what you are willing to live with. As you look at the interplay of how the alternative impacts the collective, you clarify the BATNA. Keep in mind, the extent of how far you are willing to go in each of the six pillars will help clarify which alternative is best. Following this process ensures that you do your due diligence for those heavy choices. For example, if you are trying to decide if a new job offer is the best alternative, the money might be great, and your work-life might improve, but—and this is the *big* but—it will take you away from being able to see your kids play sports, which is not acceptable. Question Seven is about as close to a 360-degree walk around as you can get.

Question Seven is my go-to for task-oriented choices, too. Using the 7MQ for alternatives that have a short-term impact is as easy as playing to your strengths, considering what you are willing to live with along the continuum from "completely not done" to "absolutely perfect." The concept of "good enough" helps you create reasonable and manageable expectations. Among equally High-Value/High-Effort tasks, a look at the available time, money, and energy (a mini look at the pillars) helps you determine what to do first, especially when everything "seems" important. "What matters most right now?" is the task-oriented version of Question Seven. Zero in and do that. Once you have dealt with the best alternative, then focus on the next best by asking the question "What matters most now?" again, over, and over, as you gradually guide yourself into alignment with your Personal Core Foundation.

Whether it's choosing among heavy alternatives or mundane daily tasks, the value of 7MQ is that you can bring your full attention to what is at hand. You develop a laser-like focus, eliminating the chatter from your mind with the assurance that the next most important item will arise. Your best mindful self is fully present for what matters.

It is my sincere hope that you use the 7MQ frequently. The discernment that arises from the process of the 7MQ is a mindfulness skill. Seeing and recognizing patterns around you for what they are, is a mindfulness skill. Accepting what is happening is a mindfulness skill. Knowing what to anticipate and how to act is the fruit of this mindfulness skill. Each of the 7MQ nudges you along to develop discernment, the process of truly being selective as to which alternative is best in any given moment. Eventually, this present moment awareness becomes a habit of being open to appreciate the fleeting moments of Augenblick that make life worth living.

Exercise #11—The Best Alternative

This exercise is designed to help you to use your intuition to choose the best alternative when there a several High-Value/High-Effort choices. However, it can be used anytime a strategic choice needs to be made.

Instructions

This exercise is entirely done by visualization and looking inwardly for the options that best resonate with the current moment. When items of equal merit and effort are considered, this technique can be used.

Exercise #11 The Best Alternative

Sit comfortably in a chair with your feet flat on the floor. Bring to mind two options with equal merit. I invite you to close your eyes and visualize a gauge similar to a fuel gauge. The indicator dial is pointing toward the left at empty. Let's call that "No." Ask yourself, "Is this the best alternative? " and see whether the indicator moves toward the right. Let's call the far-right side of the gauge "Yes." If the gauge has moved at all, see how far it registers, 10 percent, 50 percent (straight up and down), or further to the right toward 100 percent.

Repeat the question for the second alternative: "Is the second alternative the best?" Observe how far the indicator moves on the gauge. Before your finish and move on, there may be an even better alternative you haven't yet considered.

Ask one final question: "Is there a better alternative than either the first or second? Is something else better?" You can go back to your Value/Effort grid to see if something else stands out. Repeat the visualization, asking, "Is the third alternative the best option?" If you have a clear hit of 100 percent, then you have your answer—this alternative matters most right now. Otherwise, take the option that has the highest positive value on the gauge and go with that.

Reflections on Exercise #11

The choice is usually quite clear. It's rare to see a tie using this technique. No matter what, you cannot go wrong because your original intention was to choose from among items with equal merit, so taking action is better than inaction. You can always change your mind.

I highly recommend using this technique to answer the dreaded question, "Where do you want to go for dinner?" The next time this happens, close your eyes, visualize the gauge, and in under thirty seconds, your intuition will give clear a clear choice. You'll thank me but thank your intuition.

USING THE 7MQ

The Seven Mindful Questions:

1. What am I doing right now? (Awareness)
2. Why am I doing this at all? (Because)
3. Why do I care about this? (Care)
4. *Pause and Breathe.* What else should I be doing? (Pause)
5. Choose: What is essential? (Choose)
6. What can I do better? (Better)
7. What is the best alternative? (Alternative)

I'm Aware Because I Care.
Pause and Breathe.
I Choose a Better Alternative.

The Robust Application of the 7MQ

"Great questioning, great awakening;
little questioning, little awakening;
no questioning, no awakening."

—Ancient Zen Saying

I'm Aware Because I Care. ★Pause and Breathe.★ Choose the Better Alternative.

The Seven Mindful Questions are as simple as our ABCs. By now you have memorized this saying and have a working knowledge of the depth of each of the questions. My hope is that you will discover a wide range of personal applicability using this simple summary of the 7MQ. When you stop yourself in your tracks and start running the questions, you can quickly pivot to a higher value action. The 7MQ are meant to enliven your self-inquiry, paying attention to how you feel with each answer. In a discourse on Zen questioning on dharmanet.org, *"The most important thing in Zen questioning is for the question to remain alive, for your whole body and mind to become a question. In Zen [sic], they say that you have to ask with the pores of your skin and the marrow of your bones."* Open your awareness to ask with your whole being, and the innate wisdom that arises from paying attention to the response to the Seven Mindful Questions is the goal.

You will find these questions applicable in most areas of your life. You may even want to start trying them at various points throughout your day as a self-check. The use of the 7MQ is a journey into deeper and deeper personal insight.

There are multiple ways that you can work with the 7MQ, from making snap decisions in the moment to long-term planning. Here are the most common ways to start using the 7MQ in your daily life. Remember that you can always use the 7MQ when you are experiencing a stressful moment. It's easy to jump right into the questions. With practice, you'll find that you are running the questions:

- when you get up in the morning,
- mid-morning, when you need clarity on the day,
- when deciding what to make for dinner,
- during longer range planning like quarterly or semi-annually,
- anytime you want to check-in with yourself,
- and to see if you are in alignment with your Personal Core Foundation.

Example 1: Planning the Week

On Saturday mornings, I do an exercise to plan my week that includes using the ABC-Pause-CBA of the 7MQ. Saturday is an ideal day for me because I can do the planning exercise with no distractions, interruptions, or other infringements on this priority. Find a day that works best for you, where you, too, can be focused on the planning with fewer distractions. I am usually well rested on Saturday mornings. So, with a clear head, I begin to look at everything that needs to be done in the upcoming week.

During weekdays, I work full-time for a large corporation, and I have a few other activities that I block on my calendar, like exercise and evening classes. Then, I look ahead to see what time is available to work on "my stuff." My passion is writing and meditating. I start each day with a thirty-minute writing session, where I let all the morning thoughts find a way out of my head and onto paper. Then, I meditate for at least thirty minutes every morning. I note these recurring activities in shorthand on my planner.

I start thinking about activities using the 7MQ: This week, I want to get (describe the action) done, because (reason). I care about this (action) as it is (describe the feeling or what need it is fulfilling). I usually start with one big goal for the week, a goal that will take several days to complete. I know that my most productive time is in the morning. So, I look at my biggest goal, and I start planning: *This week, I want to get the Heart Centered Retreat landing page done because I would like to attract students to this event. I care about the retreat, as I am building a virtual retreat business, and this is a major life goal in alignment with my Meditation Personal Core Foundation.* There are four other areas in my Personal Core Foundation where I use this same process: Medication Consultations, Essential Oils Business, Leading Meditations, and Writing. I write them out in the same fashion: *This week I want to….* Doing this serves two purposes. First, it allows me to see the current status of each areas of my Personal Core Foundation, and, next, it allows me to see when *and if* it will be practical to actually work on that area in light of everything else going on.

Some weeks, it is easy to stage the most important goal. Other weeks, it takes several rounds of the 7MQ to get a solid plan in hand. For example: I know that the retreat is coming up, so it is easy to say, "This work needs to be done this week." I complete the *This week I want to…* statements for the retreat, but it's not my only High-Value/High-Effort priority. I complete the statement for each of my side-hustles. If I don't get the instant, intuitive "yes" hit as I'm writing the statement, I cross out the "This week" and change it to "This month" or "This quarter" or "This year." Working on a landing page for Medication Consultations, leading a sangha, and teaching an essential oils class are priorities for this month, but they are not the best use of my time this coming week. As I write out each statement, the priority becomes clear, and I can assign them to the High-Value for this week's Value/Effort grid. I know that all of these are important and will rise in priority as other time-bound tasks are completed. When I was younger, I made sure I touched on each pillar of my Personal Core Foundation every single day. I'm not that young anymore, and my ambitions have shifted. I don't want to stretch myself too thin and experience the overwhelm and burnout I felt in 2020. This year is about self-care. Evaluating what can get done on the top priority items without pushing myself too hard is an ongoing learning process for me. Underpinning that is the need to make better choices to take better care of myself. Using the 7MQ has allowed me to slow down to appreciate priorities and effort so that I can enjoy life along the way.

So now that I have addressed the Personal Core Foundation—the most important actions for the week—I move on to the Pause and "What else should I be doing?" This is where I spend some time thinking about the major self-care activities that I need to do and things that just need to be done (essentials like mowing, paying bills, cleaning the house). I have financial goals for 2021, and each week I monitor my progress in reducing spending and saving more. In January 2021, I added "menu planning" for the first time to the Saturday planning list. I do try to put one self-care and one essential activity on each day's plan so that I pay better attention to those, as well.

Things start to take shape with this iterative process of shuffling priorities. Choices based on the Value/Effort grid are staged at the Better day and time, with top priority given to the best Alternatives. I either directly enter them on a calendar time slot or I am listing them at the top of the day for flexibility. (Get it done today. The scheduled time is not important.) By the way, all my scheduling is done on paper and in pencil so that I can move things around as needed. Use what tool works for you.

At the start of each day, I look at what I have planned for myself before I do my daily writing practice. I look to see if the plan is still reasonable based on what is scheduled, what other commitments I have, what came up since I wrote the plan, and, most importantly, how my body feels. Using the 7MQ in the moment as described above, I make adjustments daily. At the end of the week, I look to see how well I did. If I stayed true to working on the goal for the highest priority, I reward myself. Something small will do, like a Friday after-work trip to Disney Springs for retail therapy. (I have the under $20 treats all scoped out if you're interested.)

Example 2: Plan Your Morning—7MQ on the Fly
Most people have multiple competing priorities in the morning. This can lead to stress and less than mindful

behavior due to the time crunch. Using the 7MQ can diffuse the stressful moments. Set the intention to have a lower stress morning. A quick rundown of the ABC-Pause-CBA in rapid succession can help smooth out your morning. Start by asking: "What am I doing right now?", "Why am I doing this?", and "Why do I care about this?" in rapid-fire succession to reset. If it's helpful, you may close your eyes so that the answers come quicker.

This gets you to the Pause and Breathe step pretty quickly. That's where you start to think about what else you should be doing in the next hour (or if that's too long, think in fifteen-minute increments). Stop your list at three things—otherwise, you'll get overwhelmed. Staging only three things allows you to move seamlessly to the next most important item. At this point, something else usually pops into my head as a "Better," so remaining flexible in the morning rush is important. Shuffle the priority so that the most important three are your focus. I finish with "What is the most important thing for me to be doing right now?" as I am already moving to the first item on my list.

All of this takes less than a minute, with way less morning-rush stress when you focus your attention on the most important task. The other "should" tasks can be organized with a repeat of the 7MQ, as soon as the first three tasks are completed. Good morning to you! Don't forget to Pause and Breathe.

Note Well

With the regular use of the 7MQ, I have been able to weed out most of the time wasters in my life. Even my downtime is purposeful; I rest and recuperate best by just sitting and knitting or watching Netflix. What looks like wasting time to you may be very restorative for me. Choose activities that nurture, replenish, and restore you, too. Don't work too hard.

My daily use of the 7MQ includes my personal imperatives like my Personal Core Foundation goals, self-care, and essentials. It's no more complicated than that. I've eliminated most everything that is a true time waster. I recommend that you use the same categories. And mix it up every once in a while, so you can try new things. Get out of your groove. Oh, and for the love of God, plan some fun into your life—if you aren't already an awesome, fun person like me.

Using the 7MQ to Make Lasting Change

If you have ever thought: *This has got to end. I need new friends. Why does this keep happening?* Or said to yourself: "Lord, I am so ready to learn whatever lesson this is presenting," then you are ready to use the 7MQ to make lasting change. This process upgrades your life. Using 7MQ is a process, similar to negotiating a business deal. Only the personal stakes are higher—much higher. Life doesn't happen by chance. Life happens on purpose. Thankfully, this process can be learned, practiced, and deployed in the highest stakes: What is it that you want out of life? Are you ready to live on purpose? Are you living in alignment with your Personal Core Foundation?

Your issues need not be major life crises. You may not be having a health emergency or teetering on the brink of financial ruin. You may not have dysfunctional friendships or need true friends. For you, it may be a slowly progressing intellectual malaise. You realize that there is more to life. You start to wonder whether the daily grind is all there is and all that will ever be. It's not. You will reach a point of no return. A point where you decide that you are no longer going to settle. You might just be fed up and ready to move on. You are ready to move on to better and bigger things, the things that ignite a passion and feed your soul. I'm here to tell you emphatically that you can do this. I'm here to tell you there is a better life—a much better life.

You can literally question yourself into a better life. The genesis of the Seven Mindful Questions was a continual negotiation to get out of bed in the morning and only do the most important task of the day. I asked myself these questions an infinite number of times until I figured out what mattered most and what I was willing to live with in terms of getting anything done. I repeated the seven questions over and over, and literally questioned myself into a much better now. If you start using the 7MQ as an ongoing internal conversation, you can, like me, question yourself into a more meaningful life.

We started early on enumerating the ways that mindfulness combined with the Seven Mindful Questions will help you in countless ways if you:

- are working from home and managing work, children, spouse, and general day-to-day life,
- are flummoxed by competing priorities,
- wonder how you will get everything done personally and professionally,
- are an individual contributor and manage your own schedule,
- work in teams where each person has responsibilities for their part of the project,
- need more structure,
- have trouble developing or keeping a routine,
- want to improve your emotional intelligence,
- are committed to improving yourself,
- want to show up as a better version of yourself every day,
- and, most importantly, help you see what really matters.

As I reflect on this list of benefits of the 7MQ, I encourage you to make the 7MQ into a mindful practice. Regular use will take you from the place where you are to the place where you want to be. Checking in with yourself is mindfulness. Mindfulness can teach you how to move from that Big Life Dream to living the dream. It happens now. It happens in the now. Use the 7MQ and show up for moments of Augenblick in your life.

I'm Aware Because I Care. *Pause and Breathe.* I Choose a Better Alternative.

Heart-Centered Exploration

Every time I come to the end of a year,
I look back. To observe.
I have the clarity of 20/20 insight.
I can see clearly
Each and every time I messed up.
It was easier to remain mute
Than to argue.
It was easier to deny myself
For the sake of responsibility.
So, one day my heart just said
Enough.
And I started to pay attention.
I looked outward at everything
In my life:
Where are you living?
What line of work are you in?
What are your hobbies?
Who is sharing your life with you?
What does an average day look like?
How are you spending your time?
None of the answers made any sense.
Living full-time in an RV.
Living alone, isolated on ten acres.
None of that made sense.
Working a job where retaliation
And retribution were daily threats.
I needed to work, so I found a new job.
And the new job made more sense.

People don't leave jobs. People leave people.

Retreating into knitting and sewing

To get away from what was bugging me,

Rather than face the mess of my life head-on,

I knit up some righteous blankets, shawls, gifts.

I reasoned that I was being productive.

I was making lemonade.

I was making the best of it all,

Because I'm an optimist.

I stumbled.

I fell face down into broken glass.

And I crawled across that broken glass.

I kept going when I should have stopped.

I kept going until going was no longer possible.

That's when my heart spoke up.

That's when I started to ask myself the hard questions.

I began to look inward for answers.

That's when the Seven Mindful Questions

Became a daily process.

Nothing was making sense.

Nothing that I was doing

Was anything at all

That I cared about.

So, I took a big, giant pause.

I kept my new job.

I kept my sweet, good-natured dog.

Everything. Else. Fell. Apart.

It hurt. A lot.

But I never lost faith.

I never lost hope.

I found that I am never alone.
And I started building a new life.
One question at a time,
I came to trust the wisdom of my heart.
My heart will answer the questions.
And show me what has meaning in my life.
My sons. My sons' wives.
My grandkids.
Where I am living now in Florida,
In perpetual summer.
I'm knitting now for absolute fun.
I'm knitting because people who live up north
Need hand-knitted things.
My job is fine.
I work to find people access to Orphan Drugs.
My work has meaning and directly helps my customers.
I've been a pharmacist so long that it's second nature.
Friends. I have old and new friends.
I'm dating and I'm going dancing (in my living room right
now).
I'm taking my time with life.
I'm okay with just waking, meditating, working, and off to
bed.
It's all okay.
Each day when I run the 7MQ,
I'm answering the questions with heart.
I'm looking for the answers that nurture me.
I'm living with passion,
And I'm living with feeling.
I'm finding that when I answer

The 7MQ with love in my heart
I have come to love and honor myself.
I'm having a do-over.
I'm doing better
Than I imagined I could four years ago
When this story started to write itself.
I'm not missing my life now.
I'm not missing those moments of Augenblick.
After many years of meditating,
I'm starting a new career to teach.
I am staying true to my Personal Core Foundation.
Trust is returning to my life,
As I come to fully appreciate
Philippians 4:7
"The peace that surpasses all understanding,
That guards my heart and mind."
That is my wish for you:
That the 7MQ come to you
Just as you need them,
As they did for me.
That by using the process
Of asking questions,
You explore your heart
And find what has meaning for you.
I wish you many moments of
Augenblick.

Guided Meditation: The Seven Mindful Questions

This guided meditation walks you through the 7MQ. Visualize yourself standing on the stairs as we start through the process. Let's leave the timeframe open to allow whatever most needs your attention to appear in your mind's eye as you walk through the seven questions. This short meditation is available for download at: https://www.lisanezneski.com/seven-mindful-questions-meditations. You may find it helpful to use a voice recorder and record your own voice so that you can follow along with the cues. Now let's get ready to meditate.

• • •

Begin by finding a comfortable position in your chair, resting your feet flat on the floor and your back against the chair. Take a full deep breath, inflating the tops of your lungs, and allow your belly to rise. Let the air leave your lungs without effort. Repeat two more full deep breaths, allowing your breath to exhale without effort. Now return your breathing to normal. When you are ready, you may gently close your eyes on your next breath or cast them downward to limit visual distraction.

Rest your attention on your breath, allowing your body to breathe naturally. Feel your body in your chair and, if you are comfortable, extend an intentional grounding link to the center of the earth, securely fastening the grounding link to the center of the earth. Feel your place in your body, on this earth at this time. Feel yourself being held by the nurturing place on the earth. You are welcome to take this place on the earth at this time.

Allow yourself at least a full minute to feel grounded on the earth.

Starting from the top stair step, "What are you aware of right now?" Notice what is in your field of attention. The A of Awareness. Rest in the awareness of what is drawing your attention.

Allow yourself at least a full minute to rest in awareness.

Stepping down to the second stair step, "Is there a reason that your awareness is drawn in a particular way? Why are you drawn to this particular awareness?"

Allow yourself at least a full minute to rest in the reason you are drawn to this particular awareness. The B of Because is the reason you are drawn to this particular awareness.

Take one more step downward and notice, "Is there a feeling or emotion that the particular awareness brings up?" Rest in the awareness until an emotion or feeling arises. Now find a label or a name for the emotion and allow the emotion to be. For example, this is anger, anger. This is regret, regret. This is impatience,

impatience. *This is frustration, frustration.* Allow the emotion to arise and acknowledge it by name. This can be an "I see you" moment. The C of Caring engenders an emotion or feeling brought on by the awareness.

If at any time the emotion gets too strong, feel free to back off the intensity to a level that you can tolerate. Take a compassionate approach to strong feelings and continue to turn down the intensity to a tolerable level.

Alternately, you can lean into the emotion and observe it running its course. Breathe.

Occasionally, the first sensation is not the only sensation. There can be a deeper, hidden emotion that arises as you let the first sensation run its course. As a secondary emotion or feeling arises, investigate with curiosity and allow the secondary emotion to run its course.

As we hit the bottom step, Pause and Breathe.

Allow yourself a full two minutes of quiet awareness to integrate the feelings and let them pass without holding on, attachment, or pushing away. If thoughts arise, that is natural, and let them pass without holding on to them. Bring your attention back to the breath and the feelings that arise.

As you turn around and before you head back up the stairs, ask the follow-up question from the bottom step, "What else needs my attention?" At this time, in this life, on this earth, what else should I be aware of? Notice what arises now. Notice any thoughts, feelings, bodily *sensations, or sounds. Allow whatever arises to come and go until there is a subtle shift in your awareness.*

Step upward into a higher awareness, some may call this the higher mind. Some may call this the soul. Some may call this the still small voice that is the moral compass. Some may call this God. We are now going to ask the higher mind for guidance to not repeat patterns or recurring mistakes or problems. There are always Choices. Ask yourself for two or three choices, options that will help you learn the essential lessons that the initial problem presented. Express your sincere desire to move beyond and not repeat the pattern. Pay attention to what enters your awareness as choices. Sit with each choice, letting the choice enter your mind's eye. Breathe.

Allow yourself at least a full minute or longer to allow at least two choices to enter your awareness.

Take the next step up and ask, "What can I do better?" Sit with whatever arises. Rest in the awareness of thoughts or feelings or bodily sensations. Allow any thoughts or feelings to arise. You may want to name them. This is thinking, thinking. This is planning, this is planning. This is forgiveness, forgiveness. This is acceptance, acceptance. This is kindness, kindness. This is love, love.

Take the final step upward and ask, "What is the best alternative?" Rest in the awareness that your higher mind will help you clearly see what can be done, what should be stopped, and what should be continued but modified.

Allow yourself at least a full minute to allow whatever arises into your awareness.

Feel the best alternative. Feel the sensations that arise when you bring your best self to a situation. Allow the feelings to permeate your body. Set an intention to allow the best alternative and your best self to stay with you after the meditation ends. Breathe.

Allow yourself at least a full minute to allow your intention to integrate into your awareness.

Whether you remember each part of the Seven Mindful Questions after this meditation is not as important as going through the process itself. Thank yourself for doing this exercise today. Begin to return your attention to your body by wiggling your fingers and your toes. And when you are ready, you may open your eyes.

• • •

BONUS MATERIAL

Bonus #1:
Recipe for "Fuck the Meatloaf"

Meatloaf is one of my favorite foods, and I tend to make it several times per month, usually with the new vegetarian-based meat substitute. Note that I am gluten and poultry free, including eggs, so this recipe is a complete experiment every time I make it. Have fun experimenting.

This recipe has basically four ingredients: meat, carbs, seasoning, something wet. You can experiment to find what fits your taste.

Ingredients:

1 lb. ground meat or 1 lb. vegetarian ground meat

Crumbled crackers—a generous handful or ¼ cup of flour (I like the density of oat flour). My dad loved Ritz Crackers, but they are not gluten-free, so no Ritz here. One time, I used the ends of a gluten-free raisin bread for an awesome jolt of sweetness.

1 T. of store brand onion soup mix

¼ cup of ketchup or ¼ cup of barbeque sauce (something tomato-based)

Mix by hand, but first take your rings off.

If the mixture feels dry (if you used flour), add some milk or milk substitute gradually until the mixture feels loafy. Not too dry, not too wet. Listen, you can't make a mistake. You really can't fuck up meatloaf.

Bake 350 degrees for 30 minutes and test to see doneness (slice with a knife and check the center). Meat substitute is usually done in 30 minutes. Regular hamburger can take 45 to 50 minutes. If you are in a hurry, 10 minutes in the microwave for meat substitute, 15 minutes for ground meat.

Enjoy!

Bonus #2:
Gratitude Journaling: How to Start a Gratitude Practice

Developing a writing habit takes time and effort. To some, it comes naturally. To others like me, it's a process that requires commitment and structure. If you're unaccustomed to journaling, start by making lists with meaning. In the summer of 2016, I happened on *The Gratitude Diaries*, written by Janice Kaplan. She spent a year where she promised to look on the bright side of everything, and it transformed her life.

When I found this gratitude practice, I was living in a thirty-two-foot RV in an industrial park alongside a busy, grimy highway, and my life sucked. I thought if Janice can do this, so can I, and what do I have to lose? Rock bottom was two rungs higher on the ladder of life. I began by making lists of ten things I was grateful for. Just that. Ten bulleted items. Some of the funny ones are: coffee, pantyhose, pulling the goalie (hockey playoffs were on), $15 flat shoes, and no complaints from my ex-husband (no comment—just funny). Some of the poignant ones are: a good job, a warm bed, a quiet morning, sand under my feet, hearing my son's voice, and my grandson liked the mail I sent.

There is a preponderance of data concerning the benefits of gratitude journaling. Evidence shows that writing about positive events for six months—three good things in life—increases happiness and decreases depressive symptoms (Seligman, Steen, Park & Peterson, 2005). In this breakthrough scientific study that was cited by multiple researchers, the research team showed that a simple practice of noting the three good things that happened to them for only one week's duration had persistent benefits. If we create a gratitude habit, imagine the impact on lasting happiness through journaling.

I encourage you to start a gratitude practice.

No matter what is happening around us, one of the best ways to stay centered and grounded and find our north star is to recognize everything for which we can give thanks. Just for purchasers of this book, you can join me in the 10-Day Gratitude Journaling Challenge, where each day we will focus on something that brings joy and meaning to our lives. I typically do the challenge twice a year: the ten days leading up to Easter, and the ten days leading up to Thanksgiving. But this practice can be done anytime. Sign up here: I'm in!

Here is how the Gratitude Challenge came about. I was sitting in meditation early one June morning in 2020, about to spend the entire day in a mastermind seminar for the second year in a row. I think we can all agree that 2020 was an unexpected year and forced us to change in ways we never thought possible. I wasn't thinking about all the horrible, awful, no good things. I was thinking about all the good things that had happened over the year since the last mastermind…and a well of gratitude erupted in my heart for all the changes and good things, good people, and especially good health in the middle of the pandemic. I spent a couple of years totally isolated, so I joined groups, a lot of groups: the mastermind, an economic movement for women, a meditation group that meets on Wednesday nights, and a group of dynamic women who sell essential oils. I had connections, real and meaningful connections. So, when I started to feel grateful and when these types of emotions arise, my tendency is to write. For the next ten days, I wrote about how grateful I was for my life. So many people were suffering through the pandemic, myself included, and I had to put my life into perspective. I was objectively doing better than I had in many years. Then, I realized that by sharing this practice, it could be much more meaningful, especially if a group of people are all doing the Gratitude Challenge together. No matter your difficulties in life, there is always a reason to give thanks.

When a group of people get together, the energy multiplies. There is power in numbers. The power behind a group being grateful will magnify, amplify, and reinforce everyone's efforts. Ten days consistently will encourage non-linear, hockey-stick-shaped, Covid-curve growth in gratitude—but this time for the good. A 10-Day Gratitude Practice will remind us to take inventory of everything that God has provided and allow us to acknowledge all the good—even now (and especially

now) in the middle of a world-wide struggle. Gratitude =
Grace.

The more you recognize and are thankful for your
life, the more grace enters your life. Try it and see for
yourself. By signing up for the challenge, purchasers of
this book get another bonus: a free downloadable 10-Day
Gratitude Journal. (link to journal). The instructions in
the challenge provide you with a different prompt each
day, encourage you to think about the prompt, feel into
it, and then write about it. Think. Feel. Write.

Each of the ten days focuses on different areas of your
life:

1. List five things that are top of mind
2. Good things
3. Bad things
4. Ugly things
5. Maslow's hierarchy of needs
6. Someone who made a difference in your life
7. Friends
8. Family
9. Your health and your body
10. Faith and hope

Bonus Exercise: Gratitude Journaling

Instructions

I hope you join me in the 10-Day Challenge. However, here is an exercise to whet your appetite and get your grateful juices flowing. For this exercise, you are going to make a bullet list of ten things that you are grateful for. Create a list of items or thoughts or people or circumstances that evoke emotion. As you write each statement, I encourage you to close your eyes and feel the gratitude.

Gratitude Journaling Exercise

Get out your journal of choice, be it electronic or paper. List ten things to be grateful for in your life. Set a timer for ten minutes and answer the following question:

What ten things are you most grateful for today?

Take your time creating the list and feeling into how grateful you are for having them in your life.

Reflections on the Bonus Gratitude Exercise

The scientific benefits of practicing gratitude through journaling include the following seven items:

1. Gratitude opens doors to more relationships
2. Gratitude improves physical health
3. Gratitude improves psychological health

4. Gratitude enhances empathy and reduces aggression
5. Grateful people sleep better
6. Gratitude improves self-esteem
7. Gratitude increases mental strength

Making a list of everything you're grateful for requires a mind shift from negative thinking to appreciation. Starting your day thinking about everything you're grateful for creates momentum in a positive direction, especially after a bad night (a bad-belly night or tossing and turning). It gets you out of "woe is me" and into a new definition of woe. Woe = Wonders Occur Everywhere. "Wow, I have enough, I am enough, I am healthy." When you are motivated to rise above the circumstances of your life, you can use the mindful journal as a tool for growth. I recommend expressing gratitude as a wonderful place to start, especially if you're unaccustomed to spilling your heart out. Like riding a bike, it takes a few awkward tries before you master the coordination of noticing a thought and capturing it on paper. The more time you spend appreciating the abundance of life, the more wonderment you'll experience. Wonders do occur everywhere. Augenblick.

—The End of This Book—
Not the end of my story, for a long time yet to come.
I have a lot of unanswered questions.

Thanks for reading *Seven Mindful Questions.* Your opinion matters. I welcome an honest review on Amazon.com. Thank you in advance for your review and for sharing this time with me. Remember you are never alone and keep asking questions.

About the Author

Lisa Nezneski, BS, PharmD, BCPS, is a certified Mindfulness Meditation teacher and a leading authority in the field of Integrative Medicine, bringing the benefits of traditional medicine, meditation, and alternative modalities in a well-rounded approach to health and healing. She is a board-certified pharmacotherapist, a certified mindfulness meditation teacher, professional healthcare consultant, Botanical Medicine specialist, Reiki Master, Intuitive, author, and speaker.

Dr. Nezneski has mastered the skills of communicating wise, fact-based advice that promotes the importance of both medication and meditation in everyday health thanks to her more than thirty years of experience in the dynamic and ever-evolving field of healthcare. As a clinical pharmacist, she served as hospital administrator, strategist, and healthcare consultant to institutions and individuals. She is lovingly known as the Queen of Orphan Drugs at her day job.

She has been a Clinical Professor at Duquesne University, and was the Chief Clinical Officer of Schatz Clinical Services, a consulting company that provided pharmacy services to small hospitals and long-term care facilities. She is currently the owner of Healthy Mindful Self, an integrative medicine company that safely combines medication with natural supplements.

Dr. Nezneski received her Bachelor's degree from the University of Pittsburgh and her Doctor of Pharmacy from the University of Cincinnati. She received her Certification in Botanical Medicine from the University of Western States, an integrative health sciences university. She obtained a certificate in Leadership Essentials from Harvard Business School and a certificate in the McKesson Leadership 201 Program from the Wharton University of Pennsylvania. Her work has been published in numerous professional journals, including the *American Journal of Hospital Pharmacy*. Dr. Nezneski is a graduate of the prestigious training program Mindfulness Meditation Teacher Certification through Sounds True.

• • •

To download free meditations, go to Lisa's website at: www.lisanezneski.com.

Endnotes

What Is Mindfulness
Maurtarano, Janice. (2014). Executive Director and Founder of the Institute for Mindful Leadership. Finding the Space to Lead. https://instituteformindfulleadership.org/finding-the-space-to-lead/
Accessed 4/13/2017

Awareness
Hodnett, Edward. (1955). The Art of Problem Solving: How to Improve Your Methods. (Harper)
Matthieson, Peter. Zen Calendar Quotes for Daily Living. 2020

Exercises #1, #2, #3
Yankovic, Weird Al. Albuquerque. From the Album Running with Scissors. 1999.

Insight On Aware, Because, Care
Beauchemin, Molly. (June 26, 2020). Understanding Ho'oponopono: A beautiful Hawaiian prayer for forgiveness. https://www.graceandlightness.com/hooponopono-hawaiian-prayer-for-forgiveness
Accessed 06/27/2020

Raypole, Crystal. (April 20, 2020). 10 Emotional Needs to Consider in Relationships. https://www.healthline.com/health/emotional-needs#things-to-keep-in-mind
Accessed 10/2/2020

Guided Meditation On Quieting Your Mind
McClintock, Liam (2018). FitMind App. Retrieved from https://www.fitmind.co/fitmind-meditation-app
Accessed 06/21/2020

Care Continued
Neff, Kristin. (2020). Test your level of Self-Compassion.
https://self-compassion.org/test-how-self-compassionate-you-are/
Accessed 10/20/2020

Guided Meditation: Self-Compassion and Feelings in Your Body
Neff, Kristin. (2015) *Self Compassion, The proven power of being kind to yourself* P 12. William Morrow Paperbacks.

Pause
Wheatley, Margaret J. (2001). Can we Reclaim Time to Think?
https://www.margaretwheatley.com/articles/timetothink.html
Accessed 9/23/2020

Mindful Journaling as a Vehicle to the Pause
Khramtsova, Irina and Glascock, Patricia. Outcomes of an integrated journaling and mindfulness program on a US university campus. Rev. Psih., t. 56, nr. 3–4, p. 208–218, Bucureşti, iulie – decembrie 2010
https://www.researchgate.net/profile/Irina_Khramtsova/publication/278784987_OUTCOMES_OF_AN_INTEGRATED_JOURNALING_AND_MINDFULNESS_PROGRAM_ON_A_US_UNIVERSITY_CAMPUS/links/5585bef508aeb0cdaddf6ae6/OUTCOMES-OF-AN-INTEGRATED-JOURNALING-AND-MINDFULNESS-PROGRAM-ON-A-US-UNIVERSITY-CAMPUS.pdf
Accessed 9/23/2020

Because
Robbins, Tony. (1992) *Awaken the Giant Within.* P 347-56. Simon and Schuster.

Exercise #9 – Willingness to Change
Prochaska JO, DiClemente CC, Norcross JC. In search of how people change. Am Psychol. 1992 Sep;47(9):1102-14.

The Robust Application of the 7MQ
Ashoka. (2001) Meditation for Life. Zen Questioning.
https://dharmanet.org/coursesM/36/lifePractice15.htm
Accessed 10/2/2020

Bonus #2 Gratitude Journaling
Reference the blog post on mindful living network
MLN Staff (2017) Start a Mindful Journal.
http://www.mindfullivingnetwork.com/start-a-mindful-journaling/
Accessed 3/24/2017

Martin E P Seligman 1, Tracy A Steen, Nansook Park, Christopher Peterson. Positive Psychology progress: empirical validation of interventions Am Psychol. Jul-Aug 2005;60(5):410-21.
Morin, Amy (2014) 7 Scientifically Proven Benefits of Gratitude.
https://www.forbes.com/sites/amymorin/2014/11/23/7-scientifically-proven-benefits-of-gratitude-that-will-motivate-you-to-give-thanks-year-round/#4afbcc95183c
Accessed 9/24/2020

www.ingramcontent.com/pod-product-compliance
Lightning Source LLC
Chambersburg PA
CBHW071615030726
47598CB00001B/292